Forever

Evolution and the Quest for Life beyond Life

by

Richard W. Kropf

Kropf, Richard W., 1932-

162 pp., includes bibliography, index

ISBN-13: 978-0615719214
ISBN-10: 061571921X

First Edition, December 2012
Second (Revised) Edition, June 2014, as updated December 2017

Stellamar Publications
PO Box 315
Johannesburg, MI 49751-0315

Cover background photo by Marisa Ross
"Sunrise over the Dead Sea"

In memory of my father, Richard Bartlett Kropf (1907-1979)
and
of my cousin, Patricia Skelly Moore (1937-2005)
and
of all the others who were also honest enough,
as their lives drew to a close, to share their worries
and doubts with me regarding the promise
and hope of eternal life.

Acknowledgments

All biblical quotations are taken from the New Revised Standard Translation unless expressly noted otherwise. Quotations from Pascal's *Pensées* are from the Amazon Kindle edition published by E. P. Dutton, and from *The Beginning of All Things* by Hans Küng, as published by William B. Eerdmans, Publishers. Quotations from the works of Teilhard de Chardin are from translations published by Harper and Row, Harcourt Brace Jovanovich, Harcourt Brace, and William B. Collins and Sons Co., Ltd.

CONTENTS

Introduction   1

Chapter 1: Evolution   11

Chapter 2: Cosmic Perspectives   21

Chapter 3: The Hope of Life   31

Chapter 4: Human Nature   43

Chapter 5: Possibilities   55

Chapter 6: Spirituality   73

Chapter 7: The Wager   87

Chapter 8: Seeking Light   107

Some Final Thoughts   117

Appendix A: Christian Universalism

       and Conditional Immortality   127

Appendix B: Karl Rahner's Vision   135

Bibliography   138

Index   145

About the Author   154

Introduction to the Second Edition

As was explained in the Foreword to the 2012 edition, this short book has been nearly half a long lifetime in its making. It all began with a question from an elderly neighbor, a devout Episcopalian whose own son was a priest of that denomination. Her question was simply this: "Do you *really* think there is something we can look forward to after death?"

My own father, a sincere convert to Catholicism, had recently asked me much the same question. At that time, I was living with him while my mother lay dying in a near-by nursing home, the victim of a stroke that had left her unable to speak or to even feed herself unassisted, yet with an awareness of all that was going on around her.

My response at that time was to write, as clearly and as succinctly as possible, my own answer to my neighbor's and my father's question. It was less than one page in length, and I do remember writing that, suspecting what we then knew about the structure of the universe, and given what we already knew about the evolution of life within it, I could simply make no sense of anything unless, when it is all over, there is the possibility that humans, or at least some of them, will continue to live on in some way still unknown to us. Otherwise, in the end, nothing makes much sense, if not in terms of scientific reasoning, at least in the existential meaning of that word. If you want to know the overall thesis of this book — or sum it up in a few sentences — it remains simply that. All the rest is simply exploring the evidence for and implications of this in our lives and whatever is to come.

So why have I waited until now, over thirty years later, to finally write this same thesis in more detail? There are two reasons for this: one is that the major difference between then and now is that the implications of what was then still called "the Big Bang theory", especially regarding the future of the universe, are now virtually certain, in contrast to back in the 1970s, when all this was still being hotly debated among scientists. One of my goals back then was to live long enough to see whether or not these speculations turned out to be fact, so much so that toward the end of the 1990s, when the first scientific indications that the Big Bang is accelerating rather than slowing down, a finding made possible by the latest generation of astronomical telescopes began to accumulate, I began to sketch out the core layout or outline of this book. But for some reason or another, probably due to more specifically Christian theological issues that I was busy addressing at the time, the project was put aside.

So again, after all this postponement, why finally now? It — and this is the second reason for it being now — is that it probably is now or never. In the late 1970s, when those first questions were asked of me, I was still busy teaching, and even if that was only part-time, it was frequently at several institutions at once. After both my parents died, I sold their home and in 1981 retired to the woods of northern Michigan to live a life of prayer, reflection, and writing. And

Introduction

among the other things, besides building, with a few friends' help, my own cabin, was to finally build, in the late 1980s and early 90s, a reflecting telescope and a small observatory to house it, from which I might get a hands-on grasp or eye-ball glimpse of at least some of the vast universe the scientists are still in the process of discovering.

Then, in the first decade of the new millennium, another part of reality began to impress itself upon me, mostly the limitations of my increasing age, among them not being able to spend much time outside under the cold and dark night sky searching for other galaxies suspended in the black vastness above. It was then, about the time of my eightieth birthday that an acquaintance of mine, a physicist who works and teaches downstate, sent me his question or the questions found in Chapter 1 and which finally spurred me to getting on with this book.

As a theologian who has specialized in contemporary science, I have written this book with two audiences primarily in mind. In the first group are those, like my physicist friend — who is a believer in his own way — are rather skeptical about the whole subject of eternal life. For them I have tried to give the principal reasons why we should still take very seriously the possibility of life after death, even while confining ourselves as closely to the scientific evidence as we possibly can. For this reason I will be particularly stressing, in Chapter 1, the importance of evolution in our understanding of life, as well as death, and in Chapter 2, the psychological and philosophical implications of what we now know about the universe.

In the second group are those who claim to be more traditional believers, but who often harbor real doubts or difficulties in squaring their religious beliefs, not just with the scientific world-view, but with the doubts that so often assail people who want to believe more firmly, yet whose faith is inevitably tested, very often by confused notions regarding what they have taken to be Christian beliefs on the subject. So while those in the first group may not think need to bother themselves with these details, it just may be that they might still get a fresh look, especially when viewed from an evolutionary perspective in chapters 3 and 4, at what they may have thought were the foundations of religious faith. In Chapter 5 we will be taking a look, at least from a more catholic — that is, all-inclusive — perspective, of what our possibilities are for what religion has called "salvation" and in Chapter 6, at the generally recognized laws of spiritual growth.

Next, realizing that all that has been said previously is, as unbelievers in evolution say, "only a theory", we will take a new look, in Chapter 7, at the odds proposed by Pascal in his famous "wager" and how, in the light of evolution, they may have changed in our favor. In Chapter 8, we will consider the kind of commitment or decision-making demanded by a life which is not merely another life after death but is totally *beyond* the limitations of this life as we experience it.

Introduction

As for those who do not identify themselves with either of the two groups described above, and who are not skeptical or who have no doubts about where they are headed, I should stress that this book was not written with them in mind. It contains a radical reassessment of certain views, like the existence of a naturally immortal soul, as being neither scientifically plausible nor scripturally consistent. Instead, I will suggest that what we think of as our soul or spirit is a product of our own personal growth, which, if we properly develop or cultivate it, results in something of a capacity or a potential for life beyond this life. In this I am following both the logic of Teilhard de Chardin's vision of evolution, as well as the thought of Karl Rahner, who had an immense influence on the theological thinking that was evidenced in the Second Vatican Council, especially as to who might qualify for God's gift of eternal life. Nevertheless, should such persons be willing to run the risk of rethinking their beliefs, they may emerge with a deepened understanding of the reasons for the hope that is within them.

Finally, a few words about the subtitle of this book. Originally, Chapter 3 was the first chapter. When some friends, after reading it, suggested that instead of the word *quest* in the subtitle that the word *hope* would be more appropriate, I resisted that idea, feeling that hope alone was too passive, and even suggestive of Freud's accusation of it all being merely so much "wishful thinking". Perhaps it is, but the whole point of this book is that this hope of eternal life is a great deal more than simply that. It is a *quest*, an active effort or even a struggle to overcome the limitations of our existence.

However, this determination to stress the necessity of our own efforts in this regard, in turn, led me to rethink the initial order of presentation. I began to realize that what I was engaged in is a kind of classical dialectic, one in which the whole evolutionary outlook on reality forms the *thesis*, thus the necessity of taking up this most fundamental topic first. But then we run into the opposing *antithesis*, which in this case is the limitation to biological evolution imposed by contemporary cosmology. Hence the question, what happens when the whole universe dies?

Toward the conclusion of his massive study, *A Secular Age,* Canadian philosopher Charles Taylor came to the conclusion that modern secularity — a worldview that permeates society without any dimension of the transcendent — has actually developed in two forms. One is basically humanistic and optimistic, trusting the best in human nature will prevail over all contrary tendencies, even without any appeal to a divinity or vision of an afterlife. The other, its opposite, is pessimistic, indeed, even nihilistic, a philosophy that focuses on the worst in human nature, and even would capitalize on that element in a cynical strategy of domination, implemented by a policy of "might makes right."

Taylor, somewhat mistakenly, I think, lays the principle blame for this state of affairs on societal pressures largely caused by religious divisions within western Christianity. True, the bloody religious wars and persecutions that afflicted Europe in the wake of the Reformation gradually drove modern societies in the direction of an ever more strict separation of church from state. We have, to some extent, been forced to adopt secularity, even if only to preserve the freedom to be religious. However, the division that exists between the two varieties of secularism that Taylor describes is, I think, more directly traceable to the scientific revolution, or more exactly the conflict between the two scientific fields, evolutionary biology and cosmology, featured in the first two chapters of this book. Simply by reading the quotes that begin these two chapters will give the reader a good idea of what I mean, contrasting the optimistic picture of evolution evidenced by Charles Darwin to the pessimistic view of our future in the universe described by astronomer James Jeans. It is here that we can see the dialectical conflict between the theory or thesis of biological advance and the antithesis to this that has become even more evident in the latest cosmological predictions based on astronomy and astrophysics. I do not think that I can over-stress the importance of this scientific thinking on our beliefs and on our hopes. *Theology*, which was defined by St. Augustine as "faith seeking understanding", draws largely on a prevailing *philosophy* and its concepts for its expression. But in turn, philosophical systems are founded, more often than not, on the prevailing world-view or a *cosmology* in the widest sense of that term. For example, belief in reincarnation is typically found wherever people think of the universe as recycling itself over the course time, which, much like the seasons of the year. On the other hand, the emergence of evolutionary science has tended to bring about a rejection of that kind of thinking.

Ideally, of course, in classical dialectic, the impasse or conflict is resolved in a *synthesis*, one which is not merely a compromise. After all, what kind of a compromise is possible between the evolution of life and the destruction of the universe in which it takes place? Instead, we seek a synthesis which represents an advancement to a whole new state of being, one that transcends existence as we know it. Hence my decision to stress, in the remainder of the book, the idea of not just another "life after death", but instead a *life totally beyond life* as we experience it within the confines of space and time. In the few pages to follow, I hope to give the reader a glimpse of what may lie, not merely after, but totally beyond this life and the death that inevitably brings it to a close.

Finally, a few words about the reasons for this new, slightly expanded edition. In addition to correcting the inevitable typographic and other mistakes that are the result of being one's own proof-reader, as well as updating the scientific data with the latest information, I felt the need to add a few pages on the fascinating and somewhat provocative issues of Christian universalism and conditional immortality — the first being the theological opinion that all souls, through the grace of God, will eventually find salvation and the second being the opinion that those who fail to reach salvation will eventually cease to exist.

Accordingly, I first want to give my thanks to Reverend Robert Wild, who first called my attention to these subjects and whose request for my opinion regarding them resulted in my writing the additional material found in Appendix A. As before, I wish to thank Jozef Bicerano, who is the person who provoked the questions asked in the first chapter of this book, and whose input, both as a scientist and as interested friend, has contributed immensely to its completion.

I also owe a special word of thanks to Anthony J. Morse, who introduced me to the works of his teacher Walter Kaufmann, loaned me the massive study by Charles Taylor, as well as gave me a copy of the thick volume by Lakoff and Johnson — a book which mostly confirmed what I had been thinking for years about biology and the human mind — and whose own questioning and suggestions prompted me to return to this project.

Thanks are also due to Patrick Stonehouse, a fellow star-gazer and lover of the cosmos, who after reading the first draft, urged me to share more of my store of knowledge of the life, work, and vision of Pierre Teilhard de Chardin. Special thanks are also due to the late William Stoeger, S.J., of the Vatican Observatory and University of Arizona for his checking and making corrections on the latest cosmological data in Chapter 2. I pray that Bill, as he was known to his many friends, both in the scientific and theological communities, is now enjoying the eternal reward among the heavens he dedicated his life to exploring. Thanks are also due to Joseph Provenzano for his exacting attention to the first draft and his helpful suggestions, to Bruce Gotts and Mary Flinn for their detailed editing, to Robert Schuster for helping me pick the right title, to Charlene Ford for her help with the book description, and to my old schoolmates James Hopewell, Harold Wessell, and Leroy White for their critiques, and to Dr. Rudolf Goetz for his continued interest in my writings and for sending me his translation of Karl Rahner's final address, which I think form a fitting conclusion (Appendix B).

Last but not least, I wish to thank Marisa Ross for the permission to use her dramatic sunrise photograph taken from the World Historical Heritage site of Masada in May of 2012. This view overlooks the Dead Sea, also known, during different historical periods, as the Sea of Salt, the Sea of Lot, the Sea of Gommorah, and the Devil's Sea, and one of the lowest (-423 meters/-1300 ft.) and least lively locations (supporting little or no life except for the tourists and other visitors) on the surface of the earth. It is, I think, a fitting symbol of the finality, and perhaps the futility, of evolution unless a fresh beginning, symbolized by the sunrise, brings the promise of new life.

Chapter 1: Evolution
or
What If We Didn't Have To Die?

> Thus from the war of nature, from famine and death, the most exalted object which we are capable of conceiving, namely, the production of the higher animals, directly follows. There is a grandeur in this view of life, with its several powers, having been originally breathed into a few forms or into one; and that, while this planet has gone cycling on according to the fixed law of gravity, from so simple a beginning endless forms most beautiful and most wonderful have been, and are still being evolved.

With the above words, Charles Darwin closed his great work, *The Origin of Species,* which hit the world like a bombshell in 1859. In fact, Darwin had already reached his conclusion nearly two decades before, but as he explained in his subsequent autobiography, which was not published until after his death, he had held off the publication of his masterwork, fearing the upset that his views would cause to society and especially to religion. And in this he was prophetic, for nothing has been exactly the same since, especially when it comes to our own understanding of human nature.

Yet, at the same time, this great discovery re-emphasized the central paradox involved in the whole phenomenon of life. It is that life, as we experience it, as intelligent beings, would not be possible unless it had evolved, not just through the struggle against death in all it forms, but even through the victory of death over those forms of life less capable of advancement into a higher form of living or level of existence.

Accordingly, when not too long ago a friend asked me the question, "If people never had to die, would they think at all about God or the existence of an immortal soul?", my first reaction to this question was to admit that no, and that probably the vast majority of people would be content to eat, drink, and even be merrier than usual, confident that they would never have to die.

However, when my friend rephrased his question shortly after, suggesting that we "Imagine a planet on which no one would ever die — in such a place would anyone spend time thinking about questions such as whether there might be a god and whether life has any purpose, or would anyone have created elaborate religious systems or would anyone even seek anything at all beyond what we already have?" So I asked myself, on such a planet, would there be people at all? After all, if anything that lived never died, how could there have been an evolution of any higher form of life to begin with? Would we not just all be like singled-celled amoebas, content — assuming that amoebas could think at all — to multiply ourselves by just growing and breaking into half, each one of which would be just one more copy of ones self?

Evolution

So back to the drawing board, and let's just imagine a planet the same as ours, except for one thing, and that is that we had finally discovered a cure for death. In a world where everything living normally has to die, humans now no longer would have to worry about that ever happening to them. What then?

For one, I suspect that much of the motivation that has advanced civilization, or even increased the human population up to now, would gradually disappear. In this I'm inclined to agree with the cultural anthropologist Ernest Becker who won a Pulitzer Prize for his best-selling book *The Denial of Death* back in 1974, the same year that he himself died.

In his book Becker claimed that nearly every human activity, ranging from artistic creation through the begetting of children, the search for fame or fortune, or even the launching of wars, has its origin in the attempt, even if mostly unconscious, to escape death. And although I remember one reviewer in *Psychology Today* magazine declaring the book as being "wrongheaded", I think Becker was largely correct.

However, aside from Becker's thesis with its hidden psychological motivations, even if death were eliminated, still, given our biological drives, it stands to reason that without death we would soon have a major overpopulation problem. In fact, due to great advances in medicine and the like, the world, with over seven billion now and a predicted ten or more billion by mid-century, is close to the breaking point already. So, if no one, once born, could die, even if conditions became so bad that they wanted to die, would we not end up in a situation where life had become worse than death? This is the situation envisioned by Britain's official "Astronomer Royal", Sir Martin Rees, prompting him to write his short 2003 book with the immense title, *A Scientist's Warning: How Terror, Error, and Environmental Disaster Threaten Humankind's Future in This Century — on Earth and Beyond.*

Yet, even if we didn't end up in such a situation — indeed, Rees thinks we are being very foolish if we don't colonize Mars by 2050 — there is a lot more to it than that. Despite what most biologists say, it really does seem to me there is some kind of *élan vital* or "vital force" or "outburst" of life, driving evolution from beginning to end, as Henri Bergson, who became one of France's most celebrated philosophers, described it. Bergson's concept has often been attacked by biologists who generally label it as some kind of mystical "vitalism" and as being superfluous and suggestive of a *teleology* or goal-seeking mechanism that the evolutionary process itself can easily explain away. But I'm inclined to see the biologists as missing the point. Or as the Jesuit priest and evolutionary paleontologist Pierre Teilhard de Chardin — who greatly admired Bergson and whom I will cite more than once in this book — once noted, how can one hold for "the survival of the fittest" unless one presumes that *survival* in itself is a goal?

Evolution

If philosophers have long speculated about there being a God at the beginning, as a kind of "ground of being" to try to explain why anything exists in the first place, then it seems to me to be just as logical, at least if it can be assumed that there is reason or purpose at work in the universe, to ask if there must not be a goal of some sort toward which we all tend, whether or not we are fully conscious of it.

This goal-seeking or drive is most clearly expressed in evolutionary terms focused on the competition between individuals or even between species in the struggle for life. Nevertheless, once we reach the fullest conscious level of human existence, we still tend, whether wisely or not, to want even more, be it more wealth, more beauty, more of everything. Thus, as Immanuel Kant, certainly one of the least passionate philosophers who ever lived, wrote, in the preface to the 1787 edition of his *Critique of Pure Reason*: "It is plain that the hope of a future life arises in the feeling, which exists in the breast of every man, that the temporal is inadequate to meet and satisfy the demands of his nature."

Nevertheless, we first have to face the fact that the belief that this desire could be fulfilled might be, as Sigmund Freud, the father of modern psychiatry, claimed, in his 1927 book *The Future of an Illusion*, a tale told by nursemaids or else just the product of "wishful thinking". After all, as Einstein pointed out, if we have evolved from creatures that instinctively avoid life-threatening situations, then should we be surprised if humans, with the ability to think reflectively — or as Teilhard often put it, "to know that we know"— look for some way to avoid death and prolong our lives forever?

I still don't know what my friend, who asked me that question regarding how humans might be affected if death didn't exist, made out of my line of reasoning on this subject. I found out later that he, as a physicist, has developed a keen interest in *cryonics*, which is the idea that persons who are dying from some ailment could be frozen in such a way that they could be carefully thawed out later on after a remedy had been developed to cure whatever they had been dying from. So I suppose that if this included curing people who had been dying simply from old age, cryonics could theoretically keep us alive (or at least in an "undead" state of suspended animation) until medical science reaches the level of maturity where a person could be kept alive once he or she is carefully thawed out.

Would we really want such a life? Might we not sooner or later become bored with life as we now experience it? Might we not have evolved with the possibility of evolving even higher? In fact, the psychologist Eric Fromm suggested that it has not taken modern evolutionary thought to inspire such thoughts. For example, we have Friedrich Nietzsche's concept of the *Übermensch* or "superman". Yet Fromm found this same theme in the very first pages of the Bible, in the ambition of the first man and woman to become, as it were, "as gods", knowing both good and evil and possessing the gift of immortality.

I do not think it has been only modern evolutionary thought or psychoanalytical interpretations of the Bible that have reinforced this fact about ourselves. Some sixteen centuries ago Saint Augustine — certainly one of the most passionate of theologians—appears to have held something of a kind of dynamic view of nature when, drawing on the thought of some of the earliest Greek philosophers, he explained how each species was created in more or less of a potential state (endowed with what he termed *rationes seminales*) which would only slowly develop their full characteristics over the course of time.

Thus it may have been that Augustine saw even human nature as still in the process of development, or that it is even in some sense still incomplete. This would seem to be implied in one of his most often quoted sayings (*Confessions*, Bk. 1, Chap. 1): "Our hearts were made for you, O Lord, and they will not rest until they rest in you."

This is not to suggest that Augustine, or even Immanuel Kant, centuries later, were covert evolutionists, even though many centuries before them, a few philosophers, like Democrates (d. 370 BCE), had suggested that life had its origins in moist earth or slime. But what both Augustine and Kant were suggesting is that human beings are capable of, or even drawn toward, a higher or more perfect state of existence than we experience in this life. For Augustine the theologian, this potential was the God-given capacity for humans to be united with God. For Kant the philosopher, the emphasis, as it was for many philosophers before him, was on the survival of that component — the "soul" — that makes us human in the first place.

In contrast to the above, for the convinced evolutionist, the hope that we might possibly live forever can only be founded on the basis of the evolutionary process itself. This becomes clear in the description of evolution that was drawn up by the scientists meeting for the Darwin Centennial at the University of Chicago in 1959. On that august occasion, the assembled scientists under the persuasive influence of the biologist Julian Huxley, grandson of Thomas Huxley, who was Darwin's most vocal advocate and his staunchest defender, proclaimed that:

> Evolution is definable in general terms as a one-way irreversible process in time, which during its course generates novelty, diversity, and higher levels of organization. It operates in all sectors of the phenomenal universe but has been most fully described and analyzed in the biological sector.

Such a definition was bound to, and in fact did, generate quite an argument (Goudge, 1961). After all, not all forms of life have developed "novelty, diversity, and higher levels of organization", as Huxley and his colleagues put it. Nevertheless, it seems reasonable to expect that evolution, having given birth to life, something lasting must result from all of this. Otherwise, given all the advances in cosmology and even in biology that have taken place since then—despite recent evidence in the field of microbiology that genetic patterns, once established, cannot be reversed or undone — the belief that evolution is "irreversible" could appear to be a bit naïve. Of course, at this point in our argument, we are clearly passing beyond pure science to philosophy or even something resembling theology, a kind of scientific faith built on the belief that evolution itself will never come completely to an end.

This same sort of optimism can be detected in Bergson's writing. In the closing lines of his third chapter of his celebrated book, Bergson wrote:

> All the living hold together, and all yield to the same tremendous push. The animal takes its stand on the plant, man bestrides animality, and the whole of humanity, in space and in time, is one immense army galloping beside and before and behind each of us in an overwhelming charge able to beat down every resistance and clear the most formidable obstacles, perhaps even death.

Yet, even this stirring scenario has its limits. As Bergson reminded us in a footnote (#90) to this same chapter,

> As has been more than once remarked, life has never made an effort to prolong indefinitely the

existence of the individual, although on so many other points it has made so many successful efforts. Everything is as if this death had been willed, or at least accepted, for the greater progress of life in general.

Thus, if we take evolution seriously on its own terms, we have to face the fact that not only individual organisms within any given species must die in order for the evolutionary process to work to begin with, but that even whole species, in fact most of the species that have ever existed, have had also to become extinct over time. In other words, the evolutionary slogan "survival of the fittest", be it applied to individuals or to whole species, perhaps needs to be rephrased as a maxim, that is, as a law that dictates that, in the end, *only the fittest will survive.* Yet, at the same time, as we shall see next, it is precisely this scientific belief that life, in one form or another, will survive, that is being challenged, especially today. This challenge comes, not from the laws of biological evolution, but from *cosmology*, that is to say, what we now know about the shape and destiny of the whole universe.

Chapter 2: Cosmic Perspectives
or
What Happens When the Universe Dies?

What does life amount to? We have tumbled, as though through error, into a universe which by all the evidence was not intended for us. We cling to a fragment of a grain of sand until such a time as the chill of death shall return us to primal matter. We strut for a tiny moment upon a tiny stage, well knowing that all our aspirations are doomed to ultimate failure and that everything we have achieved will perish with our race, leaving the Universe as though we had never existed....

The words quoted above, and ascribed to Sir James H. Jeans (1877-1946), Cambridge University physicist and another of one of Great Britain's esteemed "Astronomers Royal", may vibrate with its overtones of Shakespearean drama. Yet I know of no other statement which so eloquently sums up the human predicament in the face of a universe that Jeans, although he long proposed that the universe was constantly re-creating itself, nevertheless described as being "indifferent and even hostile to every kind of life."

Astronomers and planetary scientists like Carl Saygan, tell us that life began on this planet over 4 billion years ago, and will likely cease to exist in any form after about 4.5 billion years more, when the sun enters its red giant stage and comes close to swallowing up the earth. Even if subsequent discoveries may suggest that life may have arisen on some other planets elsewhere in this vast universe, this same pattern will most likely repeat itself. Thus Jeans' prediction of the eventual extinction of the human race is in all probability correct, — not withstanding Martin Rees' dream of our finding a refuge on Mars.

Aside from this grim, even if far-off fate, it is only natural that we humans, even as individuals, should be concerned about what happens to us when we die. After all, if even supposedly "dumb" animals instinctively try to avoid death, what makes us think that we, who can consciously reflect on the inevitability and meaning of our own death, would be any different? Some may think that this concern is childish and egocentric, but without this instinctive fear existing in each one of us as individuals, no species would have survived for long. Besides, along with that concern for our own survival, there is the concern for the survival of all whom we love.

Added to these concerns there has long been another major reason for human beliefs about the possibility of, or even the necessity for, an afterlife. It has to do with our sense of justice. It just doesn't seem right that bad or disreputable people often get away with so much and that good people so often are cheated out of their just rewards in life. For no matter how convinced we may be that this world could someday be a better place, the truth remains, especially viewed from the perspective of this world only, that life really isn't very fair, and despite our best efforts, is probably fated to remain that way. So we naturally look to an afterlife to somehow even up things.

However, recently a new level of concern has begun to spread throughout the human race, a concern more universal than just our own survival as human beings or even a craving for more justice in this world. It is a question about the survival of life itself on earth, — *all* life!

Perhaps it all began with those breath-taking views of "spaceship earth" captured by the Apollo Mission astronauts between 1961 and 1975. It was only then that we could really begin to get a sense of the fragility of our planet as a haven for life. With ever more accurate instruments recording changes on the earth's surface and in its oceans and orbiting satellites detailing alarming and life-threatening changes taking place in the atmosphere, this concern can only be deepened all the more.

However, more recent space explorations, like those carried out by the Hubble Space Telescope and its successors, are having a paradoxical effect. For instead of looking back at the earth, these orbiting telescopes, along with an array of huge new earth-based optical and infrared wave instruments, are stretching our horizon of awareness on a time and distance scale barely imagined even just a few years ago.

Forever

As of the beginning of April 2017, 3,607 "exo-planets", that is, planets outside of our own solar system have been discovered, — with 51 of them within a "habitable zone", that is to say, where water can exist. Calculating from this sample obtained by the orbiting Kepler "photometer", which has been surveying only one four hundreth of the sky since its launch in March 2009, it is now being guessed that there could be at least seventeen billion earth-sized planets within our own Milky Way galaxy!

Add to this the realization, based on estimates from sample deep space surveys by the Hubble Space Telescope, that (according to the same authority's website 2008 report) there are "hundreds of billions" of other galaxies in the universe, and it is rapidly becoming impossible to believe that we are alone. And if this is the case, then we must question whether the universe really has all that much to lose if humanity some day ceases to exist.

Nevertheless, these new discoveries are leading towards an even more unsettling question, one dealing with not just our fate, or of our world, or even of life elsewhere, but of the whole universe. While the estimate of the age of the universe as being about 13.8 billion years old is virtually unanimous among cosmologists, the answer to the question of its future longevity may still vary. However, estimates based on hard science — that is, on observational astronomy and particle physics — indicate that the universe is accelerating in its expansion, apparently to the point that it will eventually be subject to a cosmic "heat-death",— a rather paradoxical term considering that eventually the universe will grow cold and devoid of energy of any sort, that is, it will reach what is described in scientific terms as a state of complete and total *entropy*. This means, in terms of the second law of thermodynamics, that the final state of the universe will be without any free energy, thus unable to sustain motion or life.

Although there still are a few cosmologists who remain advocates for a steady state or what is termed a "flat universe", or possibly, as a second best, an oscillating universe consisting of repeated big bangs, the majority scientific opinion, at least so-far, is that the universe as we know it, is eventually doomed. If that is really the case, then the only real argument remaining is when and how.

Given enough "dark or unseen matter", which is needed to explain the gravitational behavior of the observed universe, it would require about thirty to thirty-five times as much dark matter as visible matter to produce a closed universe that would eventually collapse upon itself in a catastrophic reversal of the big bang. On the other hand, we have the mysterious effect of "dark energy", a new variation of Einstein's "cosmological constant", that is needed to explain its continued, apparently even accelerated, expansion. Whether that additional force is introduced or not, all the observational data suggests that we live in an "open" universe whose infinite expansion will lead to the eventual loss of all usable energy. All that will be left are the cold dead remains of stars and assorted leftovers suspended in space. In any case, life as we know it, according to the laws of physics and biology as we presently understand them, no matter how prolonged the present "stelliferous" or star-bearing era lasts, is all eventually destined to end — even though Richard Pogge at Ohio State University estimates that this could be a thousand trillion years from now!

Having brought up this example of truly astronomical numbers (1,000 times 1,000,000,000 or one "quadrillion"?), this is probably a good time to define what we really mean by the word *eternity*. Philosophically speaking, in a tradition going back to Plato, and passed on by Augustine and Boethius, eternity, as might be guessed from the initial *ay* in the spelling of the Latin word *ay tern itaas*, means *apart* from or *without* any time, or as the philosopher Spinoza put it, "Eternity cannot be defined by time, or have any relationship to it". However, Spinoza had to admit that "If we look at the common opinion of men, we shall see that they ... confound it with duration." Hence our loose association of eternity with time-related terms like "ever-lasting" or "forever."

A similar, but more serious, confusion consists over what is truly "science". Here and there one can find some speculation about other "universes" where our laws of nature, such as Einstein's conflation of Space-Time, might not apply or where new fresh starts at life might continue on, one after another, forever and ever. However, this sort of speculation, as evidenced in such books as Stephen Hawking's *The Grand Design*, has been judged by less imaginative — or perhaps we might say, more hard-headed — scientists, such as Eric Chaisson, who rely more on what astronomers can actually detect in their telescopes, as being "science fiction".

Yet even Chaisson, despite all the observations that indicate that the expansion of the universe is presently accelerating, seems to be persuaded that we can find some kind of cosmic equilibrium, a gap between actual and maximum entropies, as a way around the apparent inevitability that entropy will eventually shut the whole universe down. Such a scenario, which he believes is consistent with information theory, postulates that even as entropy increases, organized, complex arrangements of information or "negentropy" (negative entropy) will also increase, although not at the same rate. Others have adopted or coined different terms, such as "syntropy", "extropy", or "even "entaxy" to explain the phenomenon of life. What Chaisson seems to be suggesting, or at least hinting, is that what began from apparently nothing will not entirely end that way. One might even think of this as a secular or even scientific hope for salvation.

Thus it appears that few, even among the more sober-minded scientists, are very keen on admitting anything as threatening as a big bang that might eventually be doomed, one way or another, to turn into a big disappointment, a gigantic flash in the pan of eternity's dark night. We may have begun as "stardust",— a beguiling idea surely, — but otherwise it seems that the scenario predicted by science today is that there will be no repeat of the process and we're all in danger of ending up as ashes scattered across a cold, and dead cinder drifting in space.

Such an outcome could only mean that our sense of meaning itself would become problematic and with it the very foundations of human thinking are being turned upside down. It used to be that the most fundamental question of philosophy was "Why is there something rather than nothing?"— a question that would seem to lead to belief in a Creator or at least a "prime mover" of some sort, but which busy people could quite conveniently ignore. In his own book on the question, cosmologist Lawrence M. Krauss claims that quantum physics can explain everything, and thus that literally speaking, the universe has come from nothing. But is this not an evasion of the fact that the laws assumed by quantum physics are themselves *not* nothing? Thus, like another scientist, Victor J. Stenger, who (in his website review) complained that the title of Hawking's book implies that there just might be a "designer" after all, Krauss, in his review of Hawking's book, complained that Hawking did not go far enough in his invocation of quantum physics.

Cosmic Perspectives

Yet all this argument about where the universe came from, to my mind, misses the point, at least of this book, which is to ask where the universe is headed. After all, if the universe — which planetary scientist Carl Sagan once assured us in his book on the *Cosmos* is "all that there is, or ever was or ever will be", really *is* the whole answer, then we have a major problem. Or look at it this way: would an evolution that leads sooner or later to a more or less complete dead-end, a so-called "flat universe", devoid of all life, really make any sense, at least if we can believe the description or definition of evolution (quoted in the previous chapter) that the evolutionary scientists gave us in Chicago in 1959?

Nevertheless, if we believe, as we do, or even argue, on the basis of that belief, that once the evolution of life began then it *ought* to continue to advance, then we have a problem. Given the probable fate of the universe and the end of its ability to support biological life as we know it, and that time puts a restriction on any form of life, then would not life, if it is to continue to exist, itself have to become something eternal, that is, capable of existing *apart from* or *beyond* time? If so, then the only logical way out would be some kind of existence that transcends life as we now experience it.

Does this argument *prove* that there must be some kind of life that transcends biological evolution as it has occurred on this planet or possibly elsewhere in the universe? Not really. All it does is show that the most consistent outcome of evolution within the life-generating limits of the universe calls for its possibility. No more than that. It is only a suggestion to try to make some sense out of evolution as we understand it so far. Such a suggestion or possibility remains problematic, but no more, certainly, than the idea of other universes or a so-called "multiverse". Or perhaps another way of saying it is that, instead of other universes, there is another dimension to this one, but this other dimension is not something located somewhere else out there in time or in space. Could not it already be existing instead, in some limited sense, within us, yet at the same time, because it is still in its earliest stages of evolution, just barely evident, a mere hint of a whole new world, a whole new dimension of existence, that is still waiting to be born?

Chapter 3: The Hope of Life
or
What Is There Really To Look Forward To?

> The teachings of the Lord are three: hope of life,
> the beginning and end of our faith; righteous life,
> the beginning and end of judgment; love from joy
> and gladness, the witness of the works of a
> righteous life.

I have begun this chapter with the above summary of
the teachings of Jesus found in the late first or early
second century document mistakenly attributed to
Barnabas (1:6), St. Paul's missionary companion.
This passage has long intrigued me, especially after I
became convinced that the biggest obstacle that
Christianity must overcome is the sheer number and
complexity of its beliefs.

Nevertheless, if we follow the reasoning of
"Barnabas", whoever he may have been, we see the
first two terms of the usual order of the three
theological virtues of faith, hope, and charity
reversed. Originally it was my intention to focus only
on the first of these three teachings, the hope of
eternal life, which is what most interpreters assume
the author was talking about. Otherwise, why would
he characterize this hope as being not only the
"beginning" but also the "end" of faith?

The word *end* — which here is used to translate
the original Greek word *telos* — can itself have

several meanings. One is merely temporal, that is, referring to the cessation of time. Which is true, when hope ceases, then most likely also will faith.

Another meaning refers to a conclusion or final component, in this case the final phase of history, or of one's own individual life. But there is still another meaning, one which probably comes closest to what the author of the letter meant, and that is the *aim, purpose,* or *goal* of faith, in other words, to be able to pass from a vague hope, through a firm faith, to something better, to the possession of everlasting life. So instead of thinking of hope as a product of faith, or thinking of it as some kind of weak replacement for faith, maybe we have to place it first and foremost, with the implication that without it, there also can be no faith.

In defense of this same point of view, we could also take an example drawn from the passage in First Corinthians (15:12-19), where St. Paul speaks very strongly, in what is a kind of reverse logic about the relationship of the resurrection of the just to the resurrection of Christ. In effect, he appears to be saying that if we don't believe that the just will rise — which is surely more of a hope than a belief, since it hasn't happened yet — then there is no point in believing that Christ in fact has already risen from the dead. And if that is the case, then "your faith has been in vain." And thus, Paul concludes, "If for this life only we have hoped in Christ, we are of all people the most to be pitied."

The Hope of Life

Yet, if this is really the case, then are we not opening up ourselves to the criticism that faith is nothing more than an "illusion", the product of "wishful-thinking", as was claimed by Freud in his famous 1927 book on *The Future of an Illusion*? Thus Freud, despite his admission that religion is one of humanity's highest cultural achievements, believed that religious belief now needs to be cast aside as science advances with the correct answers to the questions that formerly religion attempted to provide.

I will have more to say about this immensely influential book, although such a shrewd and admiring citric as Walter Kaufmann (1952, Section 42) felt Freud's view that this illusion was based merely or mostly on wishful thinking was far too simplistic. Instead, I will take the position that not only has religion *been* one of humanity's highest achievements, but that it *will*, precisely because of the hope it offers, *continue to be*. In fact, I will argue that nothing really worthwhile in human life or history has ever been accomplished without some strong element of *hope* — something that Kaufmann (1963, Section 98) rather strangely, steen years before the end of his life, regarded as being more a vice than a virtue!

I realize that, for some, there is a real stumbling block here. One often hears complaints from atheists and other critics of religion that believers prove themselves to be selfish or egotistic individualists when they do good or merely behave themselves to earn some reward in the next life. And do we not have to admire the self-forgetfulness, no matter how exaggerated it may seem, as expressed by St. Paul in his Epistle to the Romans (9:3) or some other great saints who went so far as to claim that they would be willing to be damned or themselves lost if thereby they could save others?

At the same time, we must admit that religion has been given a very bad reputation by those who believe, like suicide-bombing Islamic fundamentalists, that by sacrificing themselves to kill "infidels", that their own "martyrdom" will guarantee them a place in heaven. But we must ask, how is this all that different from the Crusaders who embarked on war-like expeditions in order to have all their sins, which were no doubt many, forgiven or others who have embarked on "suicide missions" for some great cause, no matter how ill-conceived it may have been?

Yet it would seem to go against reason and nature itself to think that there is something basically wrong to imagine that somehow the idea of a reward or incentive taints or destroys the value of a good deed or worthwhile action. Think about it: would people bother to eat what they need, or get enough sleep, or go through all the bother of begetting and raising children — especially if none of these activities were not pleasurable or satisfying? I very much doubt it. So too, if obeying God's commands, or just behaving as a good citizen, did not earn us it least the admiration of one's fellow believers or the respect of one's fellow citizens, I suspect that society would soon fall apart. True, some people may do these things more for negative reasons, such as fear of some punishment or disapproval, but in today's permissive society, this has become less likely than in previous times.

Granted, that such concerns for reward or worries about one's own individual destiny often have an element of self-centeredness. Historians of Western civilization tell us that before the rise of ancient Greece and Rome, most people didn't think much of their own personal identities, but mostly thought in terms of their clan, tribe, or nation. The most ancient parts of the Bible are a good example of this almost exclusively group mentality. In the biblical realm, only some of the later Old Testament books and the New Testament evidence much interest in the fate of the individual. In fact, what seems to have taken place over the past few millennia has been a slow evolution of human self-consciousness, moving from the ancient philosophical interest in what is needed in order to lead a worthwhile life, to the Christian concern to obtain life-everlasting, and finally, nowadays, to an excessive quest for personal happiness and self-satisfaction, often with complete disregard for the well-being of others. So, not all of this development has been entirely good. And I have some sympathy for those who criticize some contemporary forms of Christian piety or the kind of economic policies that seem or claim to have been partly inspired by them. That things would come to such a pass was also foreseen by Freud, who, although he saw religion as being bulwark against both nature and the self-destructive drives of humanity, also saw it as form of collective *narcissism*, in other words, a worship of one's own self as special. Freud, in the conclusion of Chapter 3 of *The Future of an Illusion* saw this self-worship especially exemplified in Western Christian civilization and more in what is now being called American "exceptionalism". Nevertheless, most people would judge the emergence of persons as individuals, along with the recognition of the basic human rights that must be accorded to each, as a positive thing.

No doubt, hope can often be misleading. Many lives have been wasted or lost, in the hopeful pursuit of goals that turned out to be false. Yet consider the alternative. How much would have been accomplished had there not been some imagined goal or purpose to spur one on? A case in point would be Columbus' discovery of the New World despite the fact that he only wished to find a short-cut to eastern Asia and thought for some time that he actually had arrived there!

Obviously, *hope*, whether misplaced or not, is a key ingredient here. Where hope is absent, so too is faith, at least in the sense of a trust or confidence that all can turn out well for us in the end. Nor is this hope exclusively a Christian phenomenon. We can also find it in the writings of the ancients who lived centuries before the time of Christ. Certainly it is to be found in Plato's famous account in his *Dialogues* (42B) of the defense and final words of Socrates, who argued that either death is an undisturbed and therefore pleasant sleep, or else an awakening to another life, and that "Which is better God only knows."

Human nature being what it is, I doubt that few in the remote past were likely to have believed in the gods, or more in one God, unless there seemed to be some advantage in believing, or if that advantage was seen in terms of this life only. Certainly this "hope for life" that Jesus appeared to offer explains, more than any other factor, the conversion of much of the ancient world in the face of brutal persecutions launched against the first Christians. Nor would the attraction of Christianity today be so strong, particularly in the developing world, where it is still growing exponentially, unless it included some sort of promise or reward for a life well-lived—this despite all the material attractions or distractions of a higher standard of living. So while it may seem that the existential *angst* and questioning that gripped the world in the dark days during and immediately after World War II may have diminished somewhat, I suspect this apparent self-content is largely an illusion. Hope, when misdirected, is the mainspring of life, and if hope is lacking, then life itself too easily becomes a burden, a realization that is graphically portrayed in Dante's vision of hell where a sign over the entrance bids one to "Abandon hope, all ye who enter here."

Nevertheless, the more I have thought on this subject, the more I have also seen how *love* plays a more important role.

Forever

In the quote with which I began this chapter, love is seen as the fruit of hope and faith and a life well-lived. In this case, the author was obviously thinking of love in the sense of *charity,* understood as the love of God and the love of neighbor commanded by both the Hebrew Bible and the New Testament.

That some critics of religion today find the idea that love can be commanded at all to be ridiculous probably indicates the poverty of the English language more than the confusion such language is apt to cause. It also probably explains why, as the Oxford scholar and Christian apologist C. S. Lewis explained, the Greeks had four different words to express quite different forms of love.

This is also the reason why, despite all this talk about human hope, and now love, that I decided, in the subtitle of this book, to use the word *quest* as more characteristic of the whole evolutionary process. It is more characteristic of the dynamic struggle between *eros* — not just in its narrow sexual sense, which is only one aspect of the instinctual drive for life or existence — and *death,* which was one of the great themes of governing Freud's view of human psychology. As it was expressed in Part VI of his 1927 book, Freud saw this conflict as operative in all forms of life and in the whole story of biological evolution. Understood this way, we can better grasp the role that both hope and faith play in human evolution.

Faith, as we shall eventually see, also has several different meanings, but in this case, what links it most closely to hope, on the one hand, and to love on the other, is the meaning of its Hebrew counterpart *emunah*, with its emphasis on God's *faithfulness* and the New Testament emphasis on faith as a *loving trust* in God in return.

All this adds up to saying that to understand, if merely on a psychological level, the dynamics of faith, hope, and love, one must look at the last. Or as the French scientist, Pascal — of whom we will see much more later — said centuries ago, "The heart has reasons of its own" (*Pensées*, 227; 283-284)

When all is said and done, the key to the quest for eternal life is not just wishful thinking about something better — a kind of "pie in the sky when we die". Instead, it is one manifestation of a biological, fundamental physical, force, the *élan vital* about which Bergson wrote so eloquently in his book on *Creative Evolution*, despite his mechanistic critics.

It could be that these critics had also failed to take into account the larger picture as well. In that same footnote quoted (in Chap. 1 of this book) from Chapter 3 of his book, Bergson — speaking of the end of our own solar system — wrote, "Beside the worlds which are dying, there are without doubt worlds that are being born." True enough, but in the first half of the 20th century, neither Bergson, who won a Nobel Prize in 1927, nor his critics, could be expected to have a complete picture of the whole cosmos or universe.

In fact, as we have just seen in the previous chapter, until Edwin Hubble's observations with the then giant Hooker 100 inch telescope on Mt. Wilson were conducted during the years 1922-28, almost everyone thought that our galaxy, "The Milky Way" was the extent of the whole universe. Only a few more speculative characters, like the philosopher Immanuel Kant, had already, back in 1755, suggested that some of these strange fuzzy clouds or "nebulas" might be other "island universes".

Although the Russian scientist Alexander Friedmann had already mathematically demonstrated, in 1922, how Einstein's equations logically led to an expanding, and then possibly collapsing, universe, and in 1927 the Belgian physicist and clergyman, Georges Lemaître, had begun to advance the idea of the universe expanding from a "primeval atom", Einstein apparently was unaware of the first and ignored the latter. It was only after Hubble's discoveries that many of the supposed nebulas were actually other galaxies, and later in that same decade, especially his measurements of their "red shifts" indicated that most of these other galaxies were racing away from our location in space, that our present understanding of the expanding universe became generally accepted. Einstein had to modify his own theory of General Relativity, which prior to that had a "cosmological constant" figured into it to account for the belief, which turned out to be mistaken, that the overall shape of the universe always had been and always will be the same — an idea that, according to his latest biographer, Einstein admitted later was "the biggest blunder he had ever made in his life" (Issacson, 2007, p. 356).

So were Freud, who died in 1939, or Bergson, who died in 1941, aware of the implications of all of this for our understanding of our own place in the evolution of life and of the universe? If Freud was, apparently he decided to ignore it and confine himself strictly to what he believed were psychological phenomena within the human mind. Nor would it be surprising if he chose to ignore it, considering that some cosmologists, such as Fred Hoyle of Cambridge — who coined the phrase "The Big Bang" as a term of ridicule — were resisting the whole idea, until the 1990s.

I have continued to stress this whole story of scientific advancement as an object lesson in how resistant we are so often to new ideas, particularly if they threaten our sense of meaning or, perhaps more, our sense of self-worth. This explains, more than any appeal to a literal understanding of the Bible, the opposition of churchmen centuries ago to the ideas of Copernicus and the discoveries of Galileo, which together effectively dethroned humanity from its imagined center stage place in the universe. So too, the resistance to Darwin's ideas, especially when his 1859 book on *The Origin of Species* led quite logically to his 1871 book on *The Descent of Man.* (One can only wonder: might not the reactions have been somewhat different had Darwin used the word *ascent* in the place of *descent* in the title of that latter work?)

Forever

In much the same way, I think we can also explain the psychological resistance to the idea of a universe that is, to all appearances, continuing to expand towards a state, if not quite of total nothingness, nevertheless will be unable to support life in any form that we know of. From this dilemma, the dreams of other universes or a "multiverse" are born, based mostly on mathematical flights of fancy more than on the basis of any hard scientifically testable evidence.

The reason for all this is quite easy to see. Once we have lost the hope for a future life for ourselves, we seek to find some hope for the lives of others for generations to come, if not for our own descendents, for the future of intelligent life somewhere else in the universe. And while there may well be such life on some far distant planet — indeed, I'm convinced that the odds in favor of this possibility are overwhelming — still, such life would also face the same cosmological limits that we do. So while such aspirations for lives or other species other than our own are generous and noble, they are, I think, largely futile. They are, much like Freud's opinion regarding religion, yet another example of "wishful thinking".

Nevertheless, it is this aspiration or hope that leads us directly to the subject of the next chapter, where the knowledge of our evolutionary origins challenges ancient and cherished ideas about our nature as human beings and our hopes for the future.

Chapter 4: Human Nature
or
What about Us Might Be Immortal?

…what an absurd thing life is, looked at superficially: so absurd that you feel forced back on a stubborn, desperate faith in the reality and survival of the spirit. Otherwise — were there no such thing as the spirit, I mean — we should be idiots not to call off the whole human effort.

The above words (Teilhard, 1962, p. 202) were written back in 1934 by Pierre Teilhard de Chardin in a letter to the paleontologist Abbé Henri Breuil. The occasion was Teilhard's grief over the sudden death of his Canadian colleague, Davison Black, when he and Black had been working together in the same laboratory in Beijing where they were analyzing the fossilized remains of what was then called *Sinanthropus* — now classified as *homo erectus pekinesis* and thought to have lived about half a million years ago.

Even if we were to believe in the overall irreversibility of evolution — which is surely a kind of scientific faith — still, there is no hard scientific evidence that would seem to give us much hope for any personal immortality or life after death. After all, it is usually argued that if whole species have died out, and that the mechanism of evolution within a species requires death, what makes us think that we ourselves as individuals can possibly live forever? Yet, contrary to such an argument, belief in or hope for some kind of life after death has been an almost universal human phenomenon.

Historically speaking, there have been basically two major forms of belief in the afterlife. Most ancient peoples believed that all living things, including plants and animals, possess "souls" that are supposed to explain how things come to be alive and retain life. This belief, generally termed "animism" by anthropologists, has generally been thought to represent the beginning stage of religion. But as our understanding of nature increased, and this belief in everything having souls became less credible, philosophical arguments were developed to defend belief that at least humans possess a soul or spirit, enabling them, unlike mere animals, to survive to live in some sort of future life, either in a heaven, or else again on earth in another body. There have been countless variations of this belief, and despite the ascendancy of modern science, it still persists among many, maybe most, people today.

One of the few exceptions to this ancient view was to be found among the ancestors of the Jewish people whose scriptures still give us the grim warning that "You are dust and to dust you shall return" (Gen 3:19). In fact, strictly speaking, there wasn't a word in biblical Hebrew corresponding to the idea of an immortal soul. Despite the frequent appearance of the word "soul" in most English translations of the Bible, the ancient Hebrews had no concept of or even a distinct word for what the Greeks called *psychē* or "soul"— particularly as any kind of immortal spiritual substance that can survive death, or perhaps even pre-exist birth, as Plato and most of his followers understood it to be. However, Aristotle, his best-known pupil, seems to have had a somewhat different concept of the soul, which for him was more or less synonymous with the principle of life that gave form (*morphē*) to matter (*hylē*), take away that "form", and you only have dead, and eventually, unorganized matter left.

In contrast to either Plato or Aristotle, the Hebrews spoke of the *nephesh*, which originally meant a "living being" or "self". The word has also been associated with the idea of desire or thirst as well as "throat" (as in the opening verses of both Psalms 42 and 63), in which case the dynamic and still incomplete or unfulfilled aspect of the living being or self is all the more evident. Apparently, like so many other Hebrew words that began as physical terms (e.g., *ruach* or "wind" eventually meaning "spirit"), the word *nephesh* (or *nefesh*) only gradually, in more recent times, has come to mean "soul" (Alter, 2007, p. xxvii & xxviii).

Far from being the cause of life, the *nephesh* could only exist as a result of God breathing his *ruach*, ("breath" or "wind"— hence "spirit") into the human body, which otherwise, like that of the animals, was but mere *bashar* or even dead "flesh".
In fact, so down-to-earth is the biblical view of human nature that when the idea of another life after death

first entered the Bible, it was strictly in terms of God's spirit breathing directly into the same body that had died and bringing it back to life, hence the idea of a *resurrection.*

How literally this image or hope was to be taken was, even among the Jews of Jesus' time, a topic of intense debate. Extensive passages in the synoptic gospels (Mk:18-27; Mat 22:23-33; Lk 20:27-40) give the impression that while the Sadducees and other Jewish conservatives rejected the idea of resurrection, the Pharisees very much believed in it. Moreover, from the evidence provided by the Dead Sea Scrolls, the third significant religious party existing at the time of Jesus, the Essenes, believed in an angel-like existence after death. This could be very significant in view of Jesus' words "they shall be as angels", as recorded in the above-cited passages and growing speculation that Jesus himself, as well as John the Baptist, were in some way associated with the Essenes (Meier, 2001, p. 488-532, esp. note 90).

We also know that, prior to that time, certain Greek ideas about the existence of an "immortal soul" had finally begun to enter Jewish thought, as is evidenced in the *Hochma* or Wisdom writings of the Bible. Yet, this too remained controversial. Thus while the third chapter of Ecclesiastes (*Qoheleth*) evidences a rather skeptical attitude about what happens to the human "breath" when we die, its closing chapter leaves the question open.

In contrast, the later deuterocanonical — termed *apocryphal* by many — Book of Wisdom or "The

Wisdom of Solomon" (3:1-3), written in Greek by a Jew living in Egypt around the time of Jesus, eagerly adopted the Greek idea of an immortal *psychē* or soul. Significantly, neither of these wisdom books speaks about resurrection at all.

Nevertheless, this controversial idea of "rising again" has become, for the obvious reason that the Apostles claimed that Jesus had risen from the dead, the primary symbol of Christian hopes in life after death as well. So too for Islam, although the Koran (Surah 4:157-158) claims that Jesus really never died but instead gives the impression that Jesus was taken directly into heaven. At the same time, within Christianity, the idea of resurrection became gradually spiritualized to the point where sometimes it has become confused with belief in a naturally immortal or indestructible soul, similar that held by the Platonists. Much the same happened within Judaism. While the famed philosopher Moses Maimonides (Moshe ben Maimon, 1135-1204 CE) listed, in his *Guide of the Perplexed,* the resurrection of the dead as being among the beliefs held by faithful Jews, nevertheless, according to Rabbi David Wolpe, in an article on the subject on *Beliefnet*, Jews, since medieval times, have continued to hold a variety of beliefs regarding the existence of a soul and how we might continue to exist after death.

Within Christianity, the tendency to reinterpret the idea of resurrection in a somewhat more spiritual manner began with St. Paul, if we can believe Luke's account of the reactions of the crowd who had listened intently to Paul when he addressed them at the Areopagus in Athens (Acts 17:22-34). Apparently these Greeks had become used to Plato's ideas of the eternal, and thus naturally immortal, *psychē* or soul. Or perhaps they were imbued with Aristotle's idea that the rational aspect of the human soul might just be able to achieve some degree of immortality, provided that, as he urged in his *Nicomachean Ethics* (Book X, Chap. 7) "...we strain every nerve to live in accordance with the best thing in us; for even if it be small in bulk, in power and worth it surpasses everything." In any case, Paul's audience seemed to be entirely mystified or even amused by the claim that Jesus Christ had been raised from the dead, especially when the Greek word for resurrection — *anastasia,* literally "to stand up (or rise) again"— may have sounded like it might be the name of a goddess! Thus, in his First Letter to the Corinthians (15:35-53) we find Paul stressing the difference between the risen body and the earthly body that was buried in the grave.

Christianity has often attempted to combine both approaches, sometimes down-playing the miraculous physical side of things, except for the temporary appearances of the risen Christ, and stressing the spiritual aspects of life after death. Yet it still calls upon the image of resurrection, not so much to paint a picture of some kind of heavenly paradise, as to reiterate its insistence on the material-spiritual unity of human nature, a point that was strongly stressed by the great medieval theologian, St. Thomas Aquinas in both his *Summa Theologica* (Part I, q. 76, 98, 102) and his lesser known *Compendium of Theology* (Chap. 168-170).

The upshot of all of this is that unless you are a religious fundamentalist, reading scripture, be it the Bible or the Koran, literally, or a Catholic traditionalist steeped in medieval theology, or perhaps one of those people who are having their body frozen in hopes that medical science will some day have the means of curing whatever ailment killed them, any literal resurrection or physical restoration to life seems highly unlikely or outright impossible. The same might be said regarding the idea of achieving "cybernetic immortality", that is, somehow reconstituting our thoughts, memories, indeed, even our personal identity, in a newly reconstituted body by means of advancing technology. Assuming that such technology requires a material infrastructure of some sort, would not such immortality be confined to the limited duration of the universe?

However, suppose we begin to rethink human nature in terms more compatible with modern science, and began to speak of soul or spirit, not as the cause of life, but as a kind of *dimension* of, or even as a *product* of, our living. In a universe were energy and matter have long been recognized to be simply two forms or aspects of one and the same thing or in a world where structural complexity is the key to understanding the phenomenon of life, does it still make sense to speak of body and mind as if they were two distinct components of life? It would hardly seem so, at least on scientific grounds. This certainly appears to be the message of such researchers and contemporary thinkers such as George Lakoff and Mark Johnson in their 1999 book *Philosophy in the Flesh*. It also seems to be implicit in the picture of the evolution of human life and thought described by Teilhard de Chardin in Chapter 3 of Part I of his great masterwork, *Le Phénoméne humain*, which was quickly translated (not entirely with complete accuracy) and published in English as *The Phenomenon of Man*. The same approach was taken by some Catholic theologians such as Robert North in his 1968 study of the implications of Teilhard's thought, and by John Dudek in his much more explicit 2001 book on the subject.

Or, again, look at it this way: from a purely biological point of view, life and all the things that go with it, such as our thoughts, our will, and even our whole sense of self, appear to be qualities, operations, or even products of cellular organization and metabolism. If so, then why speak of soul as if it were some mysterious thing or component added to us from outside? Instead, it would seem to make more sense if whatever might possibly survive death be seen as an activity or energy that is generated within us, largely dependent on the same capacities that enabled us to develop as human beings from the very start.

Likewise, from this same perspective, there can be no doubt that a truly holistic or unified view of human nature does not favor the possibility of personal reincarnation or the transmigration of souls from one body to another. Just as our personal identity takes its origins from our own particular and unique physical mode of existence in this or that place and time, so too our "soul" or "spirit"— or whatever we choose to call the possibility of our trans-material existence beyond time — must be seen as rooted in our present material existence within space-time. This fact, according to authorities such as R. Puligandla (1975, p. 226), accounts for the distinction made long ago by religious philosophers in India between the *jiva*, the lower or phenomenal soul or self which is rooted in our particular place in space and time, and the *atman*, the higher soul or transcendent self, which they hold to be identical with *Brahman*, the ultimate reality or divinity.

However, this view logically makes the idea of *reincarnation* something to be avoided as much as humanly possible, a point often ignored by those who would look on Hindu or Vedic religion as an attractive substitute for western beliefs or hopes for life after death. In fact, the Indian word for salvation is *moksha*, which literally means "release", "deliverance", or escape from this world of change or illusion (*maya*) that is part of the whole cycle that is seen to be involved with reincarnation (Baird & Bloom, 1971, p. 267).

Instead, if we are to remain grounded in the world revealed by science, we must stress the fundamental relationship between or interchangeability of matter and energy, and the resulting wholeness of human nature, if we are to ever realistically assess the possibilities of eternal life. While we tend to speak of our bodies almost as if they were not really ourselves — e.g., "My body aches all over"— too often this kind of language can serve as an evasion of reality. Nor, despite the popularity of such terminology in some spiritual and theological writing, I do not think we are "ensouled matter", nor are we "incarnated souls". Instead, it would be more logical for us to think of ourselves as this particular energy field known as "body", which is presently capable of thinking, and loving (and hurting!) and caring about the future, and which just might, *if* enough energy is directed into the task and the proper conditions are present, be capable of living, thinking, and loving beyond this present life (Provanzano, 1993, 2000).

In the same way, would it make sense any longer to speak of soul as distinct from body, or of resurrection as something that might happen to the body as somehow distinct from soul? This does not mean that it isn't the fate of our bodies — and thus of the more material aspect of ourselves — to wear out and eventually disintegrate. But on the other hand, as the spiritual side of ourselves grows, it would mean that "resurrection" would be in some sense already taking place whenever there is a continuation beyond death of that personal center of energy or field of consciousness that we call the "self".

Is such a thing possible or even thinkable? Again consider the alternative. The biologist and evolutionary philosopher, Julian Huxley, once observed, in what has become a widely cited phrase, "Man is evolution become conscious of itself." Of course, "Man" in this sense of the word (humanity or humankind) is an abstraction. Without individual human persons, individual men and women, there is no such thing as humanity. Given what we already know of the fate of the universe, then it must be that it can only be through some such process like that which I am trying to describe, that evolution, once having become conscious, can endure. So is such an outcome possible?

Thus, it was Teilhard's firm conviction that the whole process of evolution, beginning to end, and the phenomenon of life, particularly conscious life, remains unexplainable unless one assumes that what we call matter and spirit are simply two sides of the same coin or two aspects of the same "world-stuff". Or as some would prefer, considering the convertibility (according to Einstein's famous formula that $E=mc^2$) of mass to energy or vice versa, we might just call matter "congealed [in the sense of stabilized] energy". Evolution is simply the long and involved story of how the growing complexity of physical structures lead to greater and greater manifestations of consciousness, or as Teilhard wrote in his masterwork (1959, p. 165), contrasting human self-consciousness to the earlier stages leading to it: "Admittedly, the animal knows, but cannot know that it knows."

Since Teilhard's death in 1955, extensive observations and experiments, especially with higher *primates* and perhaps porpoises, may indicate that these species begin to approach, if only on a rudimentary level, this self-awareness. This would put into question Teilhard's often quoted statement. Yet, at the same time, it would help validate his emphasis on the evolution of reflective thought through the increasing complexity of the brain structure.

It is this human capacity for reflective thought or self-consciousness that, as Albert Einstein and many others have pointed out, explains our fear of death. Without that self-consciousness, we might instinctually avoid life-threatening situations, but we would have no clear idea as to why we were doing so. So it is that, in the same way, and for much the same reasons, humans seek to find ways to deny death, or if that can't be done, cling to a stubborn or desperate faith, hoping to somehow escape its consequences. Name this effort "spirituality" or "soul-making", even "soul-growing", or call it whatever you wish, it would then have to be seen as the conscious and deliberate process by which that energy which has become matter is turned into a higher form of energy, this time as a fully evolved and conscious energy that might escape or transcend death.

If this might be possible, it is only then that we might say that evolution could *remain* conscious of itself. And if this is true, then it follows that it is only through the transformation of matter into spirit that evolution might surpass the constraints imposed by space and time.

Chapter 5: Possibilities

or

Who Has a Chance of Living Forever?

Jesus said 'The kingdom of the [father] is like a certain woman who was carrying a [jar] full of meal. While she was walking [on the] road, the handle of the jar broke and the meal spilled out behind her [on] the road. She did not realize it: she had noticed no problem. When she reached her house, she set the jar down and found it empty.'

The above parable is found only in the Gospel of Thomas (97:1-4), a battered Coptic translation of which was among the Gnostic scriptures discovered in a cave near the town of Nag Hammadi in Egypt in 1945. This very much sounds like something that Jesus might have actually said and certainly fits in with his warnings about many being called, but few chosen (Mat 8-12; 22:14). If so, it is a clear warning that outward appearances, no matter how attractively packaged, can be deceptive and that those who feel that their salvation is assured because of their birthright, tradition, or membership in this or that church or religious organization may be very much mistaken. Although the kingdom of heaven may have been outwardly announced to us by God's prophets, ultimately survival beyond this life is a matter of *desire* and of what is *within*.

However, so far, we have only been talking about a *possibility*, and one that seems pretty far-fetched at that. Now we have to get down to the business of assessing the odds of such a thing ever happening, and frankly, they do not look all that good. No matter how strongly we may wish it, what we seek appears to be, strictly speaking, beyond the capacities of human nature taken all by itself, which no doubt accounts for the wide-spread skepticism that it is possible at all. However, if one takes even a quick look at some of the experiments that are being carried out in some laboratories, particularly in the field of genetic engineering, the old biblical estimate of the average life-span being "seventy years or perhaps eighty if we are strong" (Ps 90:10), may be soon out-of-date.

Yet, even if science can make possible the estimated full natural potential of possibly reaching 120 years of age or can change our genetic components so that we can start reaching the storied life span of Methuselah, we still face the apparent cosmological limits discussed in Chapter 2. So unless we were to take seriously the closed or even repeating universe scenarios that have been largely rejected by most scientists, the chances of actually living forever in the body we have been dealt by nature, even if it were to be re-engineered genetically, look astronomically slim.

This, in turn, brings up the topic of what constitutes a *person* or *self*. Suppose, for example, that the universe turned out to be closed after all, and that eons from now there was another big bang, followed by still another, and so on, so that sooner or later, all the genetic combinations were to reoccur that might produce an exact copy of ourselves, and that eventually even everything we have done in this life would be repeated in the next. This, in fact, was the scenario envisioned by the philosopher Friedrich Nietzsche in his theory of "Eternal Recurrence". Nietzsche, famous for his proclamation that "God is dead"— as well as for having died in an insane asylum — did not believe in the existence of the immortal soul either.

So all this raises some serious questions about our identity as human beings. For one, if we really have not been given a soul, but instead have to make or evolve one for ourselves, then we have to ask an even more basic question: *who* or *what* is attempting to do all these things? Even if our self-consciousness seems to be the most fundamental fact of our existence, or as the philosopher Descartes famously wrote "I think, therefore I am", could not this "I" be largely a clever illusion? Might we not really be "a bundle of sensations", a conglomeration of neurons in the brain imagining we are a "person" or "self"? In 1994 Doubleday published a book by physicist Frank Tipler titled *The Physics of Immortality*. In it Tipler explained how he believed that the concept or law of convergence-complexity leading to consciousness, if shrewdly implemented, could prolong conscious life in the universe indefinitely. However, on close reading, it appears that Tipler's hypothesis only works within the parameters of a closed universe, and depends on a definition of life and consciousness that would include computers and various devices controlled by them as living, conscious, beings. Or conversely, as the science fiction movie "Matrix" implied, we are already simply software programs trapped inside a machine!

However, returning to the realm of nature, in this case, biology, the phrase, "bundle of sensations", is usually attributed to the 18th century Scottish philosopher, David Hume. But this denial of a soul or even a core "person" is hardly even that recent. It is essentially what Siddhartha Gautama (the original Buddha) seems to have taught in his preaching of *anatta* ("no-soul") with its corresponding doctrine of "dependent origination". Thus, according to most Buddhists, everything in the universe is connected. We are, in a very real sense, the continuation of our ancestors, and consequently, our descendents are continuations of ourselves. It is not so much (at least according to the *Theravada* branch of Buddhism or "The Way of the Elders") that individual souls but rather life itself that is reincarnated (Puligandla, 1975, p. 64). The same is true as well for at least some teachers of the more wide-spread *Mahayana* variety.

Thus, it appears that the main difference between the Buddhism and the Bible is not in their views of human nature as such. It is rather in the nature of the ultimate goal of existence and the process leading to it. For the Buddhist, life, like all nature, is seen as a cycle, offering the chance to return to an original but indescribable state of *nirvana* — literally, a "blowing out", as of a candle, yet generally understood as entry into a blissful union with a greater reality (Baird & Bloom, 1971, p. 287). This greater reality itself, however, is paradoxically expressed in negative terms in which *sunyata* or "emptiness" is experienced as an infinite fullness that embraces all reality (Matsuo Abe in Cobb & Ives, 1990). Kitagawa (1974, p. 183-188), in particular, distinguishes three versions of Nirvana corresponding to the three major schools of Buddhism which are *Theravada, Mahayana,* and *Vairayana* or *Mantrayana* — the latter school exemplified in Tibetan Buddhism and the *Shingon* school in Japan. Yet all of these varieties share a common view of this ultimate goal with its promise of freedom from the cycle of rebirth and release from all suffering.

On the other hand, for the believer in the Abrahamic tradition, which in addition to Jews, includes Christians and Muslims as well, life is a pilgrimage, a one-way journey, begun in this world, but leading towards a mysterious but loving God. Among Muslim *sufis*, the most mystical branch of Islam, the individual self is seen as if it were a mere drop of water finding its way back into a vast ocean, a simile that also found in Hindu literature.

In either case, it appears that basic to both Buddhist, as well as to biblical spirituality, is a fundamental process of "letting go" or attitude of non-attachment to self so that a higher nature, the "Buddha-nature", or as Christians see it, that the "Spirit of Jesus" or of the Christ, may take it's place.

Forever

Although this may seem a bit self-depreciating, especially compared to ancient philosophical beliefs that we possess a naturally immortal soul, I believe that these views, whether based on the Buddhist understanding of human nature or on the original biblical outlook, are not only more compatible with science but with the theological understanding of the dynamics of divine assistance or "grace".

For example, take the recasting of the ancient Hebrew *bashar* + *ruach* = *nephesh* understanding of human nature into the Greek language as we find it used by St. Paul in the New Testament (Fitzmyer, 1990, 82:101-106). According to this understanding, we consist of a body (*soma*) of flesh (*sarx*) possessing *psychē* or mind (*nous*), but which, having become conscious of self, has a drive or will or a "spirit" or *pneuma* (best written with a small "s" or "*p*") to become immortal. Yet, according to Paul (Rom 8:11), this goal is impossible without the *Pneuma* — and here we'll spell it with a capital "*P*"— that same spirit, the "Holy Spirit", that raised Christ from the dead.

However, if this is true, then what really makes us think that there still might be something of our natural selves remaining after death that just might be capable of enjoying eternity? No doubt there is something of a paradox in all of this. Yet, rather than under-cutting the possibility of anyone living forever, I believe that it is this essentially illusionary nature of the self that is the *key* to understanding how the hope of somehow escaping death could ever be turned into a realistic probability of actually doing so.

I realize that what I'm saying may not be seen as welcome news in this age of intense preoccupation with the discovery, realization, and enhancement of the true, real, and even transcendental "Self" that Carl Gustave Jung liked to extol. Since then, psychology, with its endless supply of new therapies, has largely convinced us that there has to be, underneath the various layers of our social and even ideal selves, a "real self", or an "inner child" of some sort, just waiting to be reborn. Perhaps there is, but perhaps it is not quite what we imagine it to be.

No doubt, there is a basic genetic blueprint in each of us which remains intact, but there can also be little doubt that the expression of this genetic makeup has been drastically altered, for good or for ill, by the circumstances of our upbringing. Largely in response to or even sometimes as a contrary reaction to these same circumstances, we have, in turn, formed an ideal self or goal that we became determined to achieve, sometimes accomplishing all our goals, but most often with only partial success, and this often at serious cost to what our life might have otherwise been. Not infrequently, major work remains to be done.

Still, recovery of an inner child or an imagined pristine self can be at most only a preliminary step. At most, it can only be a necessary step backward before we can prepare ourselves to take a much bigger step forward over the threshold of eternity. In this case, *evolution*, by definition a process of gradual change, becomes more like a total *revolution*. And the fact that evolution appears to be headed somewhere, or seeks immortality in some way, by no means guarantees that it will be found. After all, if the basic mechanism of evolution is a kind of drive that can be characterized as "survival of the fittest", whether the fittest are individuals or whole species, it can be expected, just like the fear of death or avoidance instinct that safeguards this drive, that having this drive does not necessarily insure its fulfillment. That moths seek the moonlight only helps insure that there will be more moths, not that any of them will actually make it to the moon!

The same is undoubtedly true for us. Despite the success of our moon-shots, when it comes to this business of surviving death we remain mere creatures whose ambitions have evolved beyond our capacity to fulfill them. In this we find ourselves in a situation not unlike that told in the story of the would-be astronaut Icarus, whose home-made wings became unglued as soon as his flight exposed him to the heat of the sun.

So where does this lead us? Definitely, it seems, "back to square one", to the problem of the origin and even more, to the destiny of all things. For a theologian, this would be just the place to get involved in a long discussion over the nature of ultimate reality, the "Ground of Being" or the source of all existence, or what so many believers all too causally refer to as "God". But this may not be necessary. It is enough, I think, at this point, to recognize that even though some people may accomplish some things in life without reference to "A Higher Power", becoming immortal probably will not be one of them.

The "Higher Power" that I speak of here does not necessarily have to be understood in theistic terms, that is, in terms of a *personal* God, one in whose "image and likeness" we have been presumably made, but which all too often has been refashioned in our own image. In fact, the term "Higher Power" is perhaps the most appropriate one when the topic is *how* this goal can be reached.

Buddhism, for example, is deeply divided over the question of whether or not one can reach the goal solely through one's own efforts. The *Theravada* Buddhists, who claim to be the most faithful to Gautama's original teachings, teach that this is exactly the case, that is, that each of us, in a sense, is our own savior. On the other hand, according to most forms of *Mahayana* — meaning the "greater vehicle"— and certainly the most popular form of Buddhism, an appeal to a higher power, often personified as the Buddha himself, is considered necessary (Kitigawa, 1974, p. 174-177).

Christians might recognize this debate as another version of the old argument over the sufficiency of "grace" and the necessity of "good works". Since nearly two-thousand years of debate have not settled the question, perhaps the old adage is best kept in mind: "Work like everything depends on you and pray like everything depends on God!"— or at least

✴# Forever

on that "higher power" that is beyond the human ability to fully comprehend.

On the other hand, have I proved that there must be an eternal life? All I have proved, I think, is that if there is to be one, it can only come from a kind of cooperative effort, a keen determination, a fierce ambition or a self-conscious evolutionary drive, coupled to kind of "faith" or a stubborn belief that there has to be something more beyond death than mere oblivion. Yet maybe it cannot be too stubborn. For if the various "faiths" really have anything to teach us, it is that true spirituality demands that we must let go of our illusory self or selves — and that there are layers upon layers of them. And one of these selves is that one which incessantly demands that we know all the answers and refuses to let go of the security of the illusion that we are always right!

In this regard — and here I'm speaking of the incessant human craving for *security* — it is important that we understand the crucial difference between *faith* and *belief*. As theologian Wilfred Cantwell Smith pointed in his 1979 book *Faith and Belief,* the word *faith,* especially in the sense that it is used in the gospels, is a *loving trust* in God. It should not be confused with the *beliefs* or opinions that we hold in our minds that serve the purpose of bolstering or attempting to justify that trust. In other words, faith is mostly a matter of the "heart", while belief, or more exactly *beliefs,* are generally more a "head-trip" or a form of understanding.

✴

Possibilities

Thus, when viewed in terms of Victor Frankl's understanding of basic psychodynamics, the obsession with absolute certainty turns out to be the very antithesis of faith. Instead, when Frankl's approach is applied to the various stages of faith described by theologian James W. Fowler, we can easily begin to see the common reasons that so many persons fail to advance in spirituality or in the life of faith. As I pointed out in my 1990 book on the subject, this business of being always right or absolutely certain is one of the biggest bug-a-boos of organized religions, especially when it comes to ideas regarding the afterlife.

Take, for example, the notion of hell or eternal punishment. Almost all religions, including Buddhism, at least those forms that have included the idea of personal reincarnation — in which case one form of punishment would be to be reborn into a lower form of life — have envisioned places or various states of punishment reserved for the wicked.

Nevertheless, *theologically* speaking, there have always been serious problems with concept of an eternal "hell" as a place or state of *everlasting* punishment. This is despite the assurances of those who tell us that God never sends people to hell and that they send themselves there. Instead, it seems hard to figure how an infinitely good God could exact unending — therefore *infinite* in its own way — punishment on limited or finite beings like ourselves, no matter how bad we may have been. There appears to be a gross disproportion. This probably explains why Origen, one of the first great Christian theologians, believed that in the end, even the Devil (Satan) would be saved. This would make Origen (185-254 CE), if not a Unitarian, at least one of the first "universalists" associated with the Christian tradition. (For more about this topic, see Appendix A.)

On the other hand, *philosophically* speaking, a rigorous defense of human free will would seem to require that we have the ability to totally reject God and remain confirmed in that decision. But need such a permanent rejection presuppose or guarantee the permanence of the person who made it? If one of our basic concepts of God is "Being in itself" or the "Ground of All Being", then a total or final rejection of God would be a removal of ourselves from the realm of being or existence. Here we can easily get bogged down in some rather tricky metaphysics, as well as linguistics. However, if we accept Augustine's definition of God as "Being as such" (*ipsum esse*) or Aquinas' description of God's primary attribute is to support his own act of being (*ipse actus essendi subsistens*), then theologian Paul Tillich's understanding of God as "the Ground of Being" may not be as redundant as it first sounds. It would seem to follow, however, that there is real difference between being and existence.

In fact, the verb *exist/s* — which comes from two Latin roots, *ex* meaning "from" and *sistere* meaning to "place", "cause" or "stand"— implies a relationship of dependence on or differentiation from something else. Understood this way, it may not really be correct to say that "God exists": creatures exist, but God simply *is*. Tillich also agreed, although for slightly different reasons. However, following the logic of this language, to be totally separated from God would mean to no longer exist. Likewise, following this same logic, rather than thinking of God sending souls to hell, by severing all relationship to God, we would simply be annihilating ourselves!

However, *psychologically* speaking, it is easy to see why religion has tended to portray hell as a "place" of eternal punishment. Freud astutely observed that it is impossible for us to imagine ourselves as dead. We instead think of ourselves as if we were bystanders or onlookers at our own funeral. If one needs to be able to have an "intuition of being" to truly be a philosopher, as Jacques Maritain used to maintain, then perhaps one also has to be a philosopher to intuit the state of non-existence — if one can even think of it as a "state".

Given this difficulty, the resulting need for concrete metaphors shows up quite well in the Bible, where the abode of the dead in Hebrew is called *sheol* or "the pit", with obvious reference to the grave, or is referred to by the Aramaic word *Gehenna*, derived from the Hebrew words for the "Valley of Hinnom", which was historically Jerusalem's city dump. That such language, along with allusions to "worms" and "fire", was ascribed to Jesus (Mk 9:48) who generally taught in parables, is natural enough, especially considering that the same language is found in the very last verse of the Book of Isaiah.

It is noteworthy, however, that St. Paul, whose writings are earlier than the four gospels, never used the Greek word *hades*. The strongest term found in the Pauline writings is "eternal destruction" (2 Thes 1:9) or "perishing", "being ruined", or "destroyed" (2 Cor 2:15), all of which sound much more like annihilation than some kind of everlasting torture. After all, how can one be annihilated yet still be around to feel pain? Indeed, in light of Paul's essentially Hebraic view of human nature, the logical alternative to eternal life would be eternal nothingness.

Nevertheless, on the other hand, as Teilhard pointed out in his spiritual testimony, *The Divine Milieu* (1960, 128-129), every well-ordered community needs a dump, in this case, as "a structural element of the universe". Yet he declined to believe that any person has ever been consigned to it. Teilhard's view on this matter becomes clearer in view of his claim in *The Phenomenon of Man* (1959, p.272) or even more explicit in his 1937 essay on "Human Energy" found in the volume bearing the same title (1969, p. 160-162). All this language suggests, I think, is the human need to graphically represent what we are unable to fully grasp, not just, as Freud suggested, our own death, but even to fully understand or intuit what means even to be or exist in the first place!

However, having just dealt with this difficult matter, I think we must also deal with one other major point of contention, especially among Christians, and that is the matter of just who can be "saved". Those who lean toward fundamentalism tend to misunderstand the passage found in the Gospel according to John (3:3) that reads, "Unless you are born again through water and the Holy Spirit you cannot enter the kingdom of God."

Obviously, for Christians, the "water and the Holy Spirit" part of the saying is seen to refer to baptism. This ritual bath, symbolizing purification or rebirth, was already known to any number of religions, and played a major role in the message of John the Baptist who may have been very much influenced by the Essenes, the Jewish sect for whom such bathing appears to have been a frequently repeated ritual. It also marked the inauguration of the mission of Jesus and according to the Gospel of John (4:1), may have even been played a role in his own subsequent ministry, although none of the other gospels mention it. So the problem is not the ritual, but rather is what is meant by "the Kingdom of God".

Many believers often seem to think that this phrase means heaven above, forgetting that in much of the New Testament, and especially in Matthew's gospel — written expressly for Jews who had become Christians. In this case, the phrase "the kingdom of heaven" is often used in place of the term "kingdom of God". This substitution was apparently done in view of the Jewish reluctance to use the name of God too readily. In fact, by the time the gospels were written, the custom was never to pronounce the proper name of God, *Yahweh,* as revealed in the Book of Exodus (3:13-15), at all, this out of fear that God's name be "taken in vain", or that it would be used too casually.

Instead, if we look at the gospels as a whole, we should be able to see that what the mission of Jesus, and before him that of John the Baptist, was all about, was first to announce the arrival of God's plan for humanity, which they referred to as a "kingdom" or "reign" and as something that is supposed to take place here on earth. Otherwise, the second petition in the Lord's Prayer, "Thy kingdom come, thy will be done, on earth as in heaven" would seem to make no sense at all. Baptism, then, is first of all meant to be a sign of openly declaring oneself as member or follower of this movement to bring God's plan to fruition here on earth.

Many may argue interminably about just what this means in practice, whether it means some kind of right-wing "dominionist" design for the political order vs. left-wing "liberation theology" of economic revolution, or simply the individual internal conversion involved in taking baptism seriously. Nevertheless, it is obvious that what is meant here by "the kingdom of heaven" or "the reign of God" means publicly aligning oneself with Jesus in what Christians call the "church"— a word meaning the assembly of those called together to accomplish

God's will. But church membership is not, in itself, a promise or guarantee of salvation, nor is salvation dependent on church membership as such.

Thus, according to the Second Vatican Council (1962-1965), the possibility of salvation or the achievement of eternal life is open to all, beginning with those who are, in the Council's "Constitution on the Church" or decree titled *Lumen Gentium* (Section 16), "are related in various ways to the people of God."

These others include, first of all, Jews "to whom the testament and promise was given and from whom Christ was born …", next Muslims, "who professing to hold the faith of Abraham, [and] along with us adore the one and merciful God…" as well as all those who "in shadows and in images seek the unknown God…" or those who "strive by their deeds to do his [God's] will as it is known to them through the dictates of their conscience."

Even more surprisingly, the Council added: "Nor does divine providence deny the helps necessary for salvation to those who, without blame on their part, have not yet arrived at an explicit knowledge of God and with his grace strive to live a good life." In other words, as shocking as it may sound to pious church-goers, the Catholic Church seems to be saying that well-meaning and good living agnostics and even atheists also can be saved or reach eternal life! The rationale that is implied here is that pursuit of the good is, in effect, a search for God, even though the latter is not (yet) experienced as being a "person".

Forever

No doubt, many sincere and convinced Christians, not unlike many Muslims who believe that all "infidels" are destined for hell, will not agree with the above statement. There seems to be something strangely satisfying to some minds in believing that only they or like-thinking people alone are destined to be saved. True, the Apostle Paul, repeating the words of the prophet Habakkuk (Hab 2:4) several times, reminded us that "The just man lives by faith" (Rom 1:17 & Gal 3:11-12). However, too often, as I have already said, we have confused "beliefs" or *dogma* — Greek word that originally meant an "opinion" or a "decision" handed down by some authority — with *faith*.

Instead, a *faith*, especially in the gospel sense of a loving *trust* in God, that would pretend to have a sure and certain knowledge, thus undermining the contrast between faith and "sight" found in St. Paul (2 Cor 5:7), would hardly be faith at all. To the contrary, it becomes a worship of certitude, and idolatry of the infallible self. It is this sort of dogmatism that has given religion — and sometimes modern science as well — a bad name. Indeed, learning to live without a complete or final answer to these questions may be a major part of the process itself. Either way, whether it be through the self-giving inspired by faith, or through the process of doubt by which we lose our illusion of self-sufficiency, we must be liberated from our transient and limited self in order to find our true and lasting self as part of a greater, infinite whole.

Chapter 6: Spirituality
or
How Might Such a Transformation Happen?

I have treated hundreds of patients. Among those in the second half of life—that is to say, over 35 years—there has not been one whose problem in the last resort was not finding a religious outlook on life. It is safe to say that every one of them fell ill because he had lost that which the living religions of every age have given their followers, and that none of them, really has been healed who did not regain his religious outlook.

The above words were written by Carl Gustave Jung (1875-1961) in his 1933 book, *Modern Man in Search of a Soul*. Jung had originally trained under Sigmund Freud, but then eventually parted ways with him because of Freud's belief that frustrated sexuality is the cause of almost every psychiatric problem. Jung also rejected Freud's dismissal of religion as having largely contributed to what Jung saw as the modern neurosis or lack of a sense of meaning in our lives. Instead, Jung saw religion, or more exactly *spirituality*, as being the key to the achievement of psychological maturity.

Everything we've already considered, all the way from the origin of the universe to the evolution of humankind, suggests that the potential for life after death can only be in terms of *progressive* change during this life. Mature oak trees do not spring from acorns overnight. While there are such things as sudden conversions or change of outlook, the kind of human psychological and spiritual maturity that one could reasonably hope would make the surviving of death possible is generally the result of only many years of growth. This is not to say that some influx of divine origin could not make up for what nature lacks, for example, in the case of those who die young. But here we are trying to confine ourselves to the natural and logical order of things, as well as account for the particular sorrow that we have when a person, so full of potential, does not live long enough for that potential to be realized. The same might be said even of the death of unborn children.

No doubt it is the realization that full spiritual maturity is rarely, if ever, seen, even in older persons, something which has given rise to such ideas as a "purgatory", a state in the next life where the often unfinished business of achieving spiritual maturity is taken care of. Given the human tendency to procrastinate, this is quite understandable. All of us would like to believe there is always the possibility of a second chance. Yet no matter how comforting such beliefs might be, *psychologically* speaking, they can severely retard serious application to the task at hand.

There is a serious *logical* problem with that idea as well. When one speaks of such a concept, is not one speaking of a passage of time? Indeed, could anyone of us really undergo or experience anything that *exists outside of or apart from time* except by some kind of loose analogy with our experience of time, or in other words, with something that lasts "forever" or continues without end? So if "eternity" is, by definition, *beyond* time, while change is something that happens only *within* time, then it stands to reason that once we have died, we are beyond any capability of change, therefore of any growth. No doubt this is at least partly why some cultures came to believe in *reincarnation,* seen as a series of lifetimes in which one had successive chances to advance to higher stages of spiritual growth, or on the other hand, regress to a lower stage depending on ones behavior in a previous life. In other words, according to Joseph Kitigawa (1974, p. 118, 124), we are dealing here with ones *karma* — literally "deed' or "act"— understood as "the moral law of causation" with "its inevitable results".

It should be pointed out that here we are considering the laws of normal human development. That there may be another providential arrangement or dispensation for those who, though no fault of their own, die young or without the chance to mature, yet still find themselves alive in "heaven", is quite another matter. It is one that I will leave to pastors to try to best explain. However, returning to the more normal or less tragic course of nature, we have to realize that we all begin life as tiny bits of protoplasm and only gradually reach, over eight to nine months time, that physical stage at which we can be safely born into this world. And just as our psychological maturity takes many years to achieve, can any one seriously believe that spiritual maturity can normally take anything but a whole lifetime, or even possibly beyond even that, to achieve?

Either way, regarding reliance on a purgatory or even belief in another lifetime given to us to shape up, it should be added that *theologically* speaking, this kind of thinking could be rather presumptuous, amounting to what the prophets used to denounce as testing divine patience or "tempting God". There may well be such a perfecting stage beyond death. It just doesn't seem very wise to count on it!

This task of achieving spiritual growth, which is generally spoken of as "spirituality" today, has long been considered one of the principal tasks of religion. Regrettably, for various reasons, many religions, or at least the institutions that claim to speak for them, have often neglected to carry out this task very well. No doubt part of the reason for this is that the more established they are in a society or culture, the more the institutional energy is taken up just providing basic care for those persons, usually the majority, who are, in a sense, spiritually immature. So the institution itself becomes less attuned to, or even somewhat threatened by the challenges of cultivating a more mature spirituality. As a result, modern popular psychology — much of it prone to fads of one sort or another — and various New Age religions have tended to fill up the gap left by churches that have failed in their primary mission. Or as it has sometimes been said, "Religion is for those who are trying to escape hell: spirituality is for those who have gone through it!"

All this is unfortunate, because if you dig deep enough, you will generally find, in the depths of your own religious background, more than enough spiritual wisdom to keep you challenged with the task of growing spiritually for a whole lifetime. In fact, as Bergson insisted in his 1932 book on *The Two Sources of Morality and Religion*, both a solid religious tradition as well as the periodic refreshment of that tradition through prophecy and mysticism are necessary for advance.

Nevertheless, underneath all the varieties of spirituality, the process of spiritual growth, just like growth of any kind, is very similar. Even though this process can be divided into many stages, they all can be generally reduced to three, corresponding more or less to what we might call spiritual infancy, prime, and maturity. However, it must be stressed that this process of spiritual growth, unlike our physical growth, is *not* automatic. In fact, more than even psychological growth, we must make a sustained and consistent effort.

These three stages have been variously named in the literature of spirituality, for example, depending on how much progress one has made: thus one might be characterized as being a "beginner", an "adept", or "proficient", or, with more emphasis on the activity characterizing each, seen as being in the "purgative", "illuminative" or even "unitive" stage. In any case, regardless of the terminology used, one must progress through the following steps or tasks.

First: you must know yourself, warts and all. Self-deception, self-justification, making excuses for ones own failings, and all the other evasions of the truth, much of it caused or at least aided or abetted by compulsive activity and addictions of one sort or another, have to be squarely faced and renounced or given up. Thus, it involves a major element of "purgation" that can only come from an initial moment of truth, followed by a decision to do something about it. The traditional word for this moment was "conversion" or in the Greek of the gospels, *metanoia*, which literally translates to "change of mind".

Second: we must embark on a program of self-improvement by seeking an ideal and working for a level of performance that tries to measure up to that ideal. This involves a great deal of thought as well as practice. It means serious study, meditation on what we have studied, and constant efforts to apply the insights — thus it is called the stage of "illumination"— and applying the fruits of such study and meditation to all our duties and circumstances of daily life. When we fail to measure up to the ideal, as we all inevitably do — otherwise we're probably not human — we must not give up. This second stage is usually the longest one, and because it requires such perseverance, by far the most difficult.

Third: finally, and hopefully, one eventually reaches the stage at which some kind of real spiritual maturity, thus "unity" with God, or with whatever is considered the highest or most ultimate reality, has been achieved. Most compulsions will have been overcome, good habits will have become second nature, and a certain amount of inner as well as outer peace and wisdom will have become manifest. While idealism may still run high, at this stage there is now usually a good measure of tolerance and compassion for those who are still struggling, and a spontaneous willingness to reach out to those in need.

However, there is still more. Quite often, even in the earlier stages, there is some evidence of some occasional, even if fleeting, experiential contact with the ultimate, thus some kind of foretaste of what an afterlife might have to offer. In the Western world, this experience has often been referred to as mystical "contemplation". In Asia, the term most often used is "enlightenment". In some ways these experiences may be like the "peak experiences" described by the psychiatrist Abraham Maslow, which are not nearly as extraordinary as one might think. Or they may be even a bit like the "near death experiences" described by Dr. Raymond Moody in his book on the subject, or even more recently, by the neurosurgeon, Eben Alexander, M.D., who, after a long period of being convinced that biology explains everything, believes that his own near-death experience, which happened during a week-long coma, constitutes a "proof" that heaven exists!

However, even aside from such extraordinary "near-death experiences", so common are the more ordinary — and certainly less dangerous — peak experiences, that maybe they should be seen as incentives for greater spiritual maturity rather than evidence that it has already been achieved.

Do such peak experiences — such as feeling a certain oneness or unity with the whole universe, or with ultimate reality — really prove that there is an afterlife or an ultimate reality that people often call "God"? If by *proof* we mean a logical argument that necessarily convinces people — other than those who have actually had the experience — beyond any doubt as to the objective reality of the soul or of God, then probably not. These are, at best *subjective* experiences, about which a researcher, like Maslow, could report that many people claim to have had. As such, they might be called "intuitions of immortality" or foretastes of ultimate reality. No doubt, some will, like Sigmund Freud, who apparently never experienced one, write the whole thing off as an illusion. In fact, Freud thought that such an experience of oneness or unity, which, in his 1930 book on *Civilization and Its Discontents*, he called an "oceanic feeling", was the opposite of religious experience, which he associated with feelings of helplessness.

To be fair, however, it should be noted that in Chapter VI in his earlier book, *The Future of an Illusion*, Freud made a careful distinction between *illusions* as being different from outright *delusions*. While the latter are clearly out of touch with objective reality, the former are not necessarily so. As Freud saw it, the problem with illusions is that, on that subjective level, they remain the object or goal of *wish fulfillment*, thus, at least in the eyes of scientists, without objective or scientifically verifiable evidence. Accordingly, Freud concluded that the testimonies of those who claim to have had such experiences are of little value to those who have not had them. On the other hand, Maslow — who once admitted he'd never had one either — took the phenomenon very seriously, as any open-minded researcher should.

As for "near-death experiences"— such as seeing one's own body from a distance, experiencing the passing through a tunnel towards a bright light, etc. — there is an additional problem. No doubt these are outstandingly "peak experiences" to those who have had them and very often have changed a person's whole attitude towards death and subsequently their whole course of life.

However, the obvious flaw as a supposed proof is that they really didn't die, and that some medical researchers have argued that such experiences may be very much part of the normal physical phenomena associated with brain death. Nevertheless, in Appendix A of his 2012 book, after citing the attending physician's estimate of his having had a 97% chance of dying, Dr. Alexander rejects (Appendix B) nine different neuroscientific hypotheses as being either impossible or highly improbable in any attempt to explain his own experience.

Forever

In any case, perhaps it is needless to say that any effort to deliberately cause such an experience could be, to say the least, rather dangerous to one's health. What we can say, at most, is that such an experience is usually highly convincing to the person who has undergone it, enough so, it would seem, to prove that the process of dying need not be nearly as frightful as one might think, at least if one is well-prepared and has the right attitude.

However, it is not just a matter of physical danger. It should be cautioned that attempts to arrive at some kind of habitual enjoyment of such ecstatic experiences are what have too often given mysticism a bad name. To seek such a goal without mastery of the preliminaries, that is, without serious commitment to the first two stages of spiritual growth, is a very dangerous delusion. Thus the chemical or drug-induced shortcuts that some have used in the past to produce some kind of imagined mystical "high" deserve not only ridicule but condemnation. This temptation to try to induce or bring about mystical experiences at will is the subject of strong warnings, or outright condemnation by classical masters of the spiritual life whose writings are filled with warnings against what they call "false mysticism". Thus, to expect the reward of faithfulness without undergoing all the work and passing all the tests of what it takes, might be seen as a form of cheating. It is also a very insidious and not too subtle form of egotism when you think about it — a matter to which we will have to give special attention in the next chapter.

Spirituality

A similar confusion of ends and means concerned Viktor Frankl, the founder of the "logotherapeutic" school of psychoanalysis — the *logos* in logotherapy standing for *meaning* or purpose. So while Frankl did not go quite as far in his more well-known books as did Jung did in his prescription of religion as a cure for the "modern neurosis", nevertheless in the introduction (p.13) to the 1979 English translation of what was actually his first book — the writing of which had been interrupted by his internment in a Nazi concentration camp — Frankl defined religion as "the search for ultimate meaning" and faith as "trust in ultimate meaning."

Nevertheless, I think that the psychodynamics that are outlined in Frankl's better-known books go a long way toward explaining the pitfalls involved in spiritual growth, as well as the warnings against them. Simply put, as Frankl emphasized again and again, in every possible way, that the search or quest for happiness or fulfillment *cannot* be successful if our *own* happiness and fulfillment or the pleasure or joy that accompanies it is the primary goal of our efforts. We can achieve happiness or fulfillment only by seeking a goal that is greater than ourselves or which transcends our own happiness. This "paradoxical intent", as Frankl called it, is essential. As he saw it, Freud's "pleasure principle", the seeking of ones own satisfaction, is faulty because it is fundamentally selfish, and not only that, it turns out to be eventually unsuccessful.

Forever

As Frankl often put it in his lectures, "The 'pursuit of happiness' just doesn't work: happiness can only 'ensue'— that is, come as a by-product of the pursuit of something greater"— presumably meaning something greater than our own happiness. So, while the instinctual drive for pleasure and satisfaction may have been programmed into us by evolution to ensure that our own or the species' basic needs are met, to seek that pleasure, whether it be aesthetic, gastronomic, sexual, or whatever, simply for our own satisfaction, is a formula for eventual disaster or at least frustration.

It is this same psychodynamic of *self-transcendence* that explains how it is that, as we saw in the last chapter, the Catholic Church came to the conclusion that even atheists and agnostics, when dedicated to a goal greater than simply their own self-satisfaction, might eventually find themselves sharing the next life in the company of the saints.

This rather paradoxical possibility also throws some light on the stark warnings of the Spanish mystical theologian St. John of the Cross (1542-1591). As he summed it in his masterwork, *The Ascent of Mount Carmel* (Book I, Chap. 13:11):

> To reach satisfaction in all,
> > desire its possession in nothing.
> To come to possess all,
> > desire the possession of nothing.
> To arrive at being all,
> > desire to be nothing.

Spirituality

To come to the knowledge of all,
desire the knowledge of nothing.

To grasp St. John's meaning, however, one must understand that the "all" (*todo*) stands for the ultimate, that is God, while the "nothing" (*nada*) literally means "no [that is, mere] thing". Thus, he went on to say:

To come to the knowledge you have not,
You must go by a way you know not.
To come to the possession you have not,
You must go by a way that you possess not.
To come to be what you are not,
You must go by a way that you are not.

When one thinks about it, these stark warnings are not all that different from Guatama's (that is, the historical Buddha's) warnings against *desire* as the cause of all our suffering. But it is not a question of cultivating passivity or indifference, as Buddhist spirituality is sometimes misinterpreted to mean. Instead, as the renowned Zen philosopher D. T. Suzuki once pointed out, one can hardly dedicate oneself to the alleviation of suffering without desiring something greater. Rather it is question of ridding oneself of selfish or self-centered desire.

Nevertheless, despite all these warnings, to ignore the challenge of reaching this final stage, or to simply shrug and fain indifference, with the excuse that, after all, are not such things supposed to be left to a future life, could be a big mistake. It is one of the reasons, perhaps the major one, that religion has so often become ineffective in reaching people or has become corrupted into rival, often warring sects. Likewise, to scorn this level of spirituality as useless or impossible, or as a distraction from our real tasks in life, is foolish and ultimately self-defeating. It would be like setting out on a journey without a map or a guidebook, or even without any idea of where you wanted to end up. Without the inspiration or goal provided by this third stage, there would be no spirituality to begin with!

However, a final caution is in order here. While the first two stages may seem to be a matter of our own doing, or our own deciding to get moving on the path of spiritual development, when it comes to the third stage, we must be patient, because it is something, like *happiness* itself, which can only *happen* to us. It is not something that we can cause just by wanting it. This doesn't mean that we shouldn't prepare ourselves to be receptive, primarily by careful attention to the first two stages. But there are also many people (perhaps even most people) for whom this final stage remains elusive. Humanly speaking, the process of spiritual development must begin with us and our own determination to achieve it. Yet, at the same time, we must always remember that it is only God, or that "Power" higher than ourselves, that can bring our evolutionary potentials to their complete fulfillment.

Chapter 7: The Wager
or
What Really Are the Odds of Living Forever?

> Let us weigh the gain and the loss in wagering that
> God is. Let us estimate these two chances. If you
> gain, you gain all; if you lose, you lose nothing.
> Wager then, without hesitation that He is….there
> is here an infinity of an infinitely happy life to
> gain, a chance of gain against a finite number of
> chances of loss, and what you stake is finite.

So begins the core of the argument found in the
Pensées or "Thoughts" of the French mathematician
and scientist Blaise Pascal (1623-62). In Part III of
this notebook, which was not published until some
years after his death, Pascal pondered "On the
Necessity of the Wager" regarding the existence of
God and the fate of the soul. His argument, which
goes on at some length, is usually summarized in
something like the following paragraph.

Suppose that there really is a God who will hold
us accountable for the way we live our life. In that
case we'd better behave or we'll surely end up the
loser. On the other hand, if such a belief is an illusion,
still, when we die, what really will we have lost?
Perhaps an excuse to have lived however we pleased?
But on the other hand, if we have lived *as if* there is a
God who holds us accountable, we will have, if

nothing else, at least earned a reputation as a basically decent person.

Put in those terms, Pascal's argument is often perceived as being as cynical, insincere, or, at the most, as a very shallow form of faith. Would God really reward us for simply playing it safe? Might we not say that what we have here is not faith at all, but at best a vague hope, or at worst, venal self-promotion? Would not God, some critics ask, be justified in sending such a believer to hell as a punishment for his insincerity? (However, it strikes me as rather odd how unbelievers who often make this criticism can claim to be so sure that God, whom they do not believe in, is of such a vindictive nature.)

Instead, I would suggest that the critics need to take a much closer look at what Pascal was saying. We should especially note that he says:

> ... it is no use to say it is uncertain if we will gain, and it is certain that we risk, and that the infinite distance between the *certainty* of what is staked and the *uncertainty* of what will be gained, equals the finite good which is certainly staked against the uncertain infinite. It is not so, as every player stakes a certainty to gain an uncertainty, yet he stakes a finite certainty to gain a finite uncertainty, without transgressing against reason.

Accordingly, in the same passage of his *Pensées*, (Part III, Section 233), Pascal argued that:

The Wager

... if there are as many risks on one side as on the other, the course is to play even; and then the certainty of the stake is equal to the uncertainty of the gain, so far is it from fact that there is an infinite distance between them. And so our proposition is of infinite force, when there is the finite to stake in a game where there are equal risks of gain and of loss, and the infinite to gain. This is demonstrable; and if men are capable of any truths, this is one.

Volumes have been written, pro and con, about Pascal and his famous wager, and no doubt, the objection can been made that Pascal had in mind the traditional view of the Abrahamic faith tradition of a God who is preeminently a "person" who cares about how we live our lives and will hold each of us accountable. However, is not this same accountability also implicit in Asian views of *karma* and rebirth, even though, according to Puligandla (1975, p. 25), the ultimate reality and the law of *karma* may be seen as being impersonal?

Thus, the focus of Pascal's wager really doesn't necessarily have to be applied to the issue as to whether or not there is a personal God, but can also be applied to the question as to whether or not something of our selves — call it soul or spirit — survives the physical death of our body.

In fact, this seems to be implied when Pascal added: "And thus, when one is forced to play, he must renounce reason to preserve his life rather than risk it for infinite gain, as likely to happen as the loss of nothingness." In other words, life leaves us no choice: we are forced to choose, and *the choice of* nothingness is no more reasonable than the risk involved in believing.

However, I believe that the risk of not believing may be even *greater*. This would be because of what I suggested in Chapter 4, that we are not born with immortal souls but instead only with a spiritual capacity to grow or develop one. If so, then the risk of not believing would give new meaning to Hamlet's famous question about whether it is better "to be or not to be?" This ability to destroy our own being, thus our own evolutionary potential, would certainly be in sharp contrast to what many assume Pascal envisioned; that the penalty for wagering wrongly would be to suffer eternal torment. It would be even more in contrast to what St. Augustine believed; that the essence of this torment was to *have to be* when one wished *not to be*.

In *The Phenomenon of Man*, Teilhard mentions Pascal at least four times (1959, p. 40, 44, 217, 233) which, when taken together point out how Pascal's 17th century era physics, with his concepts of the infinitely large and the infinitely small, each reproducing the other but on a vastly different scale, were essentially an "illusion" caused by the ignorance of evolution and especially his failure to recognize the emergence of the infinitely *complex*. Consequently, according to Teilhard, Pascal's wager needs to be corrected, at least to the extent that the odds are seen as being in any sense even.

Instead, as Teilhard put it: "When one of the alternatives is weighted with logic, and in a sense by the promise of a whole world, can we still speak of a game of simple chance?"

Teilhard then moved quickly to answer that question by responding:

> The world is too big a concern for that. To bring us into existence it has from the beginning juggled miraculously with too many improbabilities for there to be any risk whatever in committing ourselves further and following it right to the end.
> (Teilhard, 1959, p. 233)

This argument of Teilhard's in some way anticipates what has come to be called the "anthropic principle", which is the much debated argument that evolution appears to have been "designed" in some way to produce intelligent life — either that, or else one must presuppose the existence of innumerable other universes to account for the slim chance that life might appear in at least one of them. Then, based on that same sort of reasoning, Teilhard pushed his argument on to a final step, asserting that, in view of the whole direction that evolution has taken so far, adding, with an eye to the future that…

> … life, by its very structure, having once been lifted to the stage of thought, cannot go on at all

without requiring to ascend even further… [and consequently]…That there is for us, in the future, under some form or other, at least collective, not only survival, but *super-life*. (Teilhard, 1959, p. 234)

Teilhard's mention of a "collective" form of a "super-life" here might suggest something like the concept of the re-absorption of the individual soul at the time of death into a "world-soul", or something like Aristotle's idea that the intellectual soul or rationality in some sense might achieve immortality. However, what Teilhard had in mind becomes clear in Book Four, where this collective is described as culminating in the "Omega-Point", which although it is already realized in God, nevertheless includes individual human consciousness, a point that he further elaborated in his 1937 "Sketch of a Personalistic Universe" (Teilhard, 1969, p. 65-71).

In any case, it needs to be remembered that fundamental to Teilhard's view is the principle that true "union"— as distinguished from mere conglomeration —"differentiates". In this case, our immortality is insured by becoming part of the larger game of life. It is not a question of absenting ourselves from the rough and tumble of life in the world, which is the impression given by Pascal's strict Jansenist piety, sometimes described as a kind of Catholic puritanism. Instead, the price that we have to pay in order to play, is, to a certain extent, to risk ourselves and the meaning of our own short life in the goal of achieving something much greater than just our own holiness or our own salvation. Either that, or the alternative is to relegate ourselves to the sidelines of evolution.

Yet, what if we don't have naturally immortal souls as something given to us, but rather have only the potential of making ourselves immortal? And then suppose the condition of such an advance is not simply our own will power but instead our conscious alignment with that creative energy that lies at the heart of the evolution or future of the Universe? In other words, suppose that what we call "ethics" or "morality" is not just a question of our behavior as individuals, or even just its social consequences, but is ultimately a matter of *love* on a much more universal scale, and, as such, is the very essence of what we have generally called "religion".

Here I would again point out that I choose to differ slightly from Teilhard in this regard. In a footnote in *The Phenomenon of Man* (1959, p. 169, n.1), Teilhard appears to have given the impression that what we call the "soul" is, in some sense, *naturally* immortal, if not exactly in the sense that Platonism thought souls to be — that is, as pre-existing spiritual entities — but rather as a natural or automatic result of the evolutionary process. However, as we shall see, certain comments (which we will see in the next chapter) that Teilhard made shortly before his death seem to indicate he was having second thoughts about this. Thus, I tend more to side with Karl Rahner (1978, p. 120-128) who saw this aspect of our human nature as an "obediential" capacity, something that is, of its nature, incomplete and remains so unless we reach out in some way toward God for its fulfillment.

This view, which Rahner often expressed in terms of humans possessing a "supernatural existential", might also explain the Vatican II teachings (quoted in Chapter 5) regarding the salvation of non-believers, with their seeking of what they believe is right and good for the world beyond what is simply for ones own selfish purposes. This seeking is, or at least in existential terms amounts to openness to God's grace with its gift of eternal life. In this aspect, Karl Rahner admitted that he was indebted to Teilhard's views, especially when it came to the subject of "hominization" or the evolution of the human species. Rahner also seems to have been influenced by Henri de Lubac, a Jesuit who was a personal friend of Teilhard, but whose views expressed in his own book on the subject of human nature and God's grace were proscribed, much like Teilhard's writings, by Roman censors back in 1950. This was particularly ironic, inasmuch as de Lubac's views were largely derived from those of the ancient Eastern Church theologians who saw human nature as incomplete and requiring God's grace before a human can achieve his or her full human capacities. De Lubac's book *Le surnaturel* was finally published with Church approval in 1964 and he has also been credited — although those who did so remain officially anonymous — with having had a large part to play in the drafting of the last (and longest) document to come out of the Second Vatican Council, known by its Latin title *Gaudium et spes* ("Joy and Hope") or more formally as the "Constitution on the Church in the Modern World". In any case, there are passages in it that resemble, almost word for word, some of Teilhard's writings.

Despite the great contrast between these three great modern Jesuit thinkers and Pascal with his 17th century physics and Jansenist sympathies — his *Provincial Letters* were particularly scathing in their criticism of what Pascal believed to be laxity in Jesuit ethical reasoning — I think that Pascal was essentially right when it comes to evaluating what is at stake in his "wager". Either we cooperate with this great creative force which we have generally, and again, perhaps too casually, called "God". Or else we can go off by ourselves to play our own little game, one which in the end, if we can believe most of the scientists as well as Pascal, will only lead, if not to actual, at least to virtual nothingness. Accordingly, given this new and greatly expanded interpretation of Pascal's wager, one in which the odds are weighted more strongly in favor of the survival of life in a "world" beyond this one, I think the words of the contemporary Swiss Catholic theologian Hans Küng are telling. As he wrote in the last part of the epilogue of his 2007 book on science and religion (p. 205-206):

I personally have accepted Blaise Pascal's 'wager' and have put my stake on God and the infinite against the void and nothingness — not on the basis of a calculation of probability or mathematical logic but on the basis of a rational trust. I do not believe in the later legendary elaborations of the New Testament message of the resurrection but in its original core: that this Jesus of Nazareth did not die into nothingness, but into God. So trusting in this message, I hope as a Christian, like many people in other religions, not to die into nothingness, which seems to me to be extremely irrational and senseless. Rather, I hope to die into the ultimate reality, into God, which — beyond space and time in the hidden real dimension of the infinite — transcends all human reason and conceiving...

Küng then continues:

Of course, I am aware of the abiding risk of this wager in unconditional trust, but I am convinced that even if I lose the wager in death, I will have lost nothing for my life; at all events, I will have lived a better, happier, more meaningful life than if I had not had hope. (Küng, 2007, p. 205-206)

I think it is significant that Küng dealt with these matters and many more surrounding the subject of death and the possibilities of an afterlife in his 1982 book titled *Ewiges Leben*? (Eternal Life?) and that we should note that the 1985 English translation bears the subtitle *Life After Death as a Medical, Philosophical, and Theological Problem*. Yet despite this extensive look at the whole subject, in this earlier book Küng does not mention Pascal's wager and in fact only mentions him once, this in regard to another author's recalling Pascal's paradoxical remark about it not needing the whole universe to kill a human and that just one drop of [tainted] water is sufficient!

Küng did, however, take a paragraph of this earlier book (1985, p. 226) to distance himself from Teilhard's view that science itself discloses an ultimate meaning to the universe. Instead, he credits Teilhard with "establishing a new understanding between theology and natural science", apparently because Teilhard had forced the Church to take evolution seriously. But in regard to Teilhard's views as to the direction evolution is taking, Küng cautioned against what he saw as an unwarranted mixing of scientific conclusions with religious convictions.

So what has taken place to explain the liberal theologian Küng turning to pondering Pascal's wager? The cynic might ascribe it to Küng being several decades older when he began to take Pascal more seriously. Or could it be instead that Küng has taken Teilhard more seriously? If his 2007 book on the subject is any indication, it appears that he has. Not that he still didn't have doubts about some of Teilhard's theological ideas, especially his almost complete avoidance of the historical Jesus. But despite these misgivings, there can be no doubt that to Küng, Teilhard has become something of a hero because of his stubborn insistence that theologians must take science seriously, even when it meant being held under suspicion by church authorities and the suppression of his writings — a fate not unlike that suffered by Küng, who was deprived of his status as the officially Church-approved Catholic theologian at the University of Tübingen.

In this latter regard, Küng singles out one of Teilhard's papers that particularly aroused ecclesiastical alarm bells. This was Teilhard's long 1934 essay on "How I Believe" (Teilhard, 1969, p. 96-132), which begins with this fourfold profession of faith:

I believe that the universe is in evolution.

I believe that evolution proceeds toward spirit.

I believe that spirit is realized in a form of personality.

I believe that the supremely personal is the universal Christ.

Then, not too much further into the same essay, Teilhard made the statement, one which particularly alarmed the Roman authorities:

If, as the result of some interior revolution, I were to lose in succession my faith in Christ, my faith in a personal God, and my faith in spirit, I feel that I should continue to believe invincibly in the world. The world (its value, its infallibility and its goodness) — that, when all is said and done, is the first, the last, and the only thing in which I believe. It is by this faith that I live. And it is to this faith, I feel, that at the moment of death, rising above all doubts, I shall surrender myself.

(Teilhard, 1969, p. 99)

What are we to make of this last statement? Taken in isolation, it certainly seems to be a rather disconcerting admission coming from a Catholic priest. Was Teilhard on the brink of losing his faith — or had he done so already? Considering the way he had been treated by the Church, one might readily understand and forgive him for walking out on it altogether. But he never did.

However, when taken in the context of the *psychological* steps through which *his* faith progressed — which he insisted that he was trying to outline in this essay — it is rather a bold statement of the foundation of where his faith began. Not that it was always so. He had grown up in a home of rather conventional 19th century French Catholic piety which, like Pascal's, was flavored with Jansenism and its overtones of *odium mundi,* which if not an outright hatred of this world, at least harbored strong suspicions of any attachment to the world as a source of corruption of the spirit and a danger to the faith. Teilhard's faith had become just the opposite. Strangely fascinated by rocks and minerals as a child — he said because of their permanence — he had rediscovered, during his early training as a Jesuit on the island of Jersey, this same fascination, but this time within the context of the geological evolution of earth and the biological evolution of life. As a Jesuit "scholastic" teaching in a Catholic school for boys in Cairo, he took his young students on trips out into the Egyptian desert to search for fossils. Later, still a yet-to-be-ordained theological student, and not yet professionally trained in the science of paleontology, he had been involved, at least peripherally, in the discovery of the fossil known as the "Piltdown Man" in a gravel pit near Hastings, England, which over forty years later, to Teilhard's chagrin, had turned out to be a hoax perpetrated, it seems, by someone with closer ties to the English scientific establishment. Nevertheless, so well-recognized was Teilhard's interest in the Church coming to grips with the challenge that evolution presented, that he was invited to write part — the part dealing with evolution (Bergson's *L'Evolution créatice* first appeared in 1907) — of a long article on "The Nature of Man according to the Teachings of the Church and the Philosophy of the Spirit" for the 1911 edition of the prestigious *Dictionaire apologetique de la foi.* So there can be no doubt of Teilhard's determination to dedicate his life to the reconciliation of religion and science.

Only if we understand all this, can we then appreciate how fundamental was his belief in evolution and the vehemence of that paragraph quoted above, which if understood in context, takes us to the next step, his "Faith in Spirit"— a *"spirit which is born within, and as a function of matter"* (Teilhard, 1969, p. 103-108).

I do not think that it is possible to overemphasize the importance of that last quoted statement if we are to understand the core of Teilhard's thinking or the evolutionary thesis that is the impetus behind the writing of this book. Even though the material and the spiritual may often seem to pull us in opposite directions — which they often do in practice, and which struggle forms the main theme of so much traditional spirituality — we must understand that the contest is not between two opposed entities, but between two vectors or directions of movement affecting a single basic thing, or what Teilhard termed (using the German word — surely a major concession for Frenchman!) *weltstoff.* In other words, it is a matter of understanding evolution in terms of the emergence of the spirit from the basic "stuff" of what is generally called "matter", which, as was explained in Chapter 4, especially in the light of contemporary cosmology, could be best thought of as a kind of a subsequent congealment of the energy released at the moment of the big bang.

In any case, it is this fundamental unity of matter and spirit that explains Teilhard's insistence that, when it comes to the evaluation of this evolution, we must hold, as an "absolute principle of appraisal" or even as "the absolute condition of the world's existence", to this maxim: "it is better, no matter what the cost, to be more conscious than less conscious." Thus, while Teilhard admitted that many people he

Forever

knew could not follow him in this belief, he laid the blame not on any ill-will on their part, but on their failure to see or appreciate the world seen as a *whole*. However, once this holistic viewpoint is achieved, then, despite all the changes and fluctuations that occur within nature, we come to the realization "that the only [i.e., constant] reality in the world is the passion for growth."

Next (Teilhard, 1969, p. 109), at least for the purpose or aim of this book, comes the most important step of all, which is "*Faith in Immortality*", which, in turn, forms the beginning of the next stage of Teilhard's understanding and presentation of his beliefs. Yet, at this point, he had to admit that what he held was more a "vision of *hope*" (emphasis mine) and that by immortality he meant, first of all "*irreversibility*" (this time the emphasis was his). Here he based his argument on what he considered to be another fundamental law within the universe and that is "if a thing is possible, it will be realized." And then, after admitting that *entropy* (again the second law of thermodynamics) still plays a role, one intensifying the struggle for life, Teilhard insisted that nevertheless *life* constantly reasserts itself.

In any case, I think it is significant that here Teilhard turned to the philosopher Maurice Blondel — whose book *L'Action* had, in 1893, caught the world's attention, as well as the Catholic Church's suspicions — and to the work of Teilhard's own friend, Édouard Le Roy, who had been a disciple of Henri Bergson, and who like Blondel, fell under the censure of the Church. Teilhard summed up their thought thus:

'If that thing, apparently so small, which we know as human activity, is to be set in motion, nothing less is required than the attraction of a result that cannot be destroyed. We press on only in the hope of an immortal conquest.' And from this I draw the direct conclusion that 'ahead of us there must therefore lie something that is immortal.'

(Teilhard, 1969, p. 110)

And what is that thing that is immortal? As he expressed it in the third item of his short 1934 profession of faith, it is *"a form of personality."* Later, to be even more specific, he modified that statement in a footnote added from his 1950 essay "The Heart of Matter". It reads, "Today, I would say, 'I believe that *in man*, spirit is fully realized in person." (Teilhard, 1978, p. 78, n.7) In other words, Teilhard believed that, from the *scientific* perspective, that reflective consciousness — to be able "to know that we know", which he saw as being the defining characteristic of human life — represents, at least on this planet, the culmination of evolution and that if evolution is to continue or even result in something lasting, it can only be in the form of the human spirit or that core of individual personhood that past ages, and occasionally even Teilhard, called "soul".

Thus Teilhard stubbornly remained committed to his vocation, not only as a scientist, but also as a

Jesuit priest who remained devoutly loyal to his vision of Christ, seen as the center of human co-consciousness, and thus also as the pinnacle of human evolution. I will not go further into this last element of Teilhard's faith, as that is not the purpose of this book, which is to strengthen the *hope* of immortality to persons of any faith or even no faith at all. But I do hope that this will show how the faith of Teilhard de Chardin was founded on the bedrock of his love for the world and his conviction that its evolution is — as the gathered scientists at the Darwin Centennial in 1959 were to say, and as Teilhard had already stressed — *irreversible.*

That conviction in itself is, I believe, to some degree, a leap of faith, and it explains why Küng, who has in some ways been treated by the Vatican much as Teilhard was, speaks of his own acceptance of Pascal's wager, not just in terms of hope, but of "trust"— which is, as we have seen, the gospel sense or the basic meaning of the word *faith.* As such it is both a "rational trust" but even more an "unconditional trust" that we "will not die into nothingness."

Although he was not speaking of religious faith in his book *Creative Evolution*, Bergson — who although he was raised Jewish, had become an atheist around age sixteen — nevertheless wrote at some length, toward the beginning of his chapter (the same as quoted previously in this book) on "The Meaning of Life", about the limitations of the human intellect and its reasoning abilities. The intellect has become, as he put it, "a nucleus formed by means of condensation", and thus, by a process of abstraction, "detached itself from a vaster reality…" So it is "of the essence of reasoning to shut itself up in the circle of the given." Thus, he described what we might even see as a vicious circle:

> So you may speculate as intelligently as you will on the mechanism of intelligence: you will never, by this method, succeed in going beyond it. You may get something more complex, but not something higher nor even something different.

What is the answer? Bergson likened the situation to the difference between walking and swimming. "Thousands upon thousands variations on the theme of walking will never yield a rule for swimming", but once you have taken the *leap* — and here Bergson actually uses that word — you will understand how "Swimming is an extension of walking."

So, as Bergson had already admitted, "there is a kind of absurdity in trying to know otherwise than by intelligence", still — and here I have added emphasis to Bergson's own words —"if the *risk* be frankly accepted, *action* will perhaps cut the knot that reasoning has tied and will not unloose." In light of this latter statement, it is understandable why Bergson, toward the end of his life, seriously considered becoming a Catholic, although he ultimately decided against it, apparently in solidarity with his fellow Jews who were being interned and even murdered by the Nazis.

Of course, one need not go to any of these more recent authors to learn what is ultimately at stake. It is not just a matter of finding the meaning of life, even it be characterized, as did Frankl, as *"ultimate meaning"*. Jesus himself put it even more starkly when he warned his followers with his question about "What does it profit...?", which when translated in terms that accord much more closely with what we learned in chapter 4 is not just (as our old renditions of Luke 9:25 had it) about losing our "souls". Instead, as the majority of our contemporary translations have it, it is a choice between gaining the whole world, but at the price of losing or "forfeiting" *ourselves*. And thus, if we were to retranslate this warning into evolutionary terms, it would be ultimately a choice between achieving our full potential as human beings or else passing away into a final state of non-existence or total nothingness.

Chapter 8: Seeking Light
or
How Shall We Decide?

Today, ninety-nine percent of men, perhaps, still fancy that they can breathe freely this side of an unbreakable death-barrier — provided it is thought to be sufficiently far away. Tomorrow (and of this I am certain because, like so many other people, I am already experiencing it) mankind would be possessed by a panic claustrophobia simply at the idea that it might find itself hermetically sealed inside a closed universe.

The above words were written by Pierre Teilhard de Chardin in the next-to-last page of a short essay titled "The Death-Barrier and Co-Reflection" which was composed a scant four months before his own death, in New York City, on Easter Sunday, April 10, 1955, but which was only published years later (Teilhard 1970, p. 397-406).

It should be understood that by a "closed universe" Teilhard was not referring to the then current debate over whether or not the universe is "open" in the sense of infinitely expanding, which is the prevailing cosmological opinion today, or else "closed" in the sense of eventually collapsing upon itself. Instead, what he meant by "closed" was that either way, the future of the universe was limited and that sooner or later the second law of thermodynamics, which applies to all "closed" or isolated systems, would have its way and *entropy* would reign supreme, that is, unless reflective thought, "knowing that we know", in some way might survive. To his mind, it was this possibility, which he saw as to some extent already taking place in the phenomenon of "co-reflection"— humans thinking together and being drawn into a greater unity — that he seemed to think that future salvation of humanity lay. It was, one might say, Teilhard's attempt to prove that there must be, if evolution itself is not to prove a failure, some kind of transcendent state awaiting us beyond. This was, as may be familiar to readers of his other writings, the ultimate or "Omega-Point" of evolution, which for Teilhard was symbolized in Christ.

Teilhard's vision of evolution and of the human phenomenon was taken up with great interest all around the world. His masterwork, *Le Phénoméne humain,* once it was published shortly after his death, was soon translated into several dozen languages — not always with complete accuracy. In fact, I can remember meeting several scientists from the Soviet Union (a year or so before its collapse in 1991) who knew of him or had read this book, although the Russian language version, at least the one published under the Communist regime, had pointedly omitted the epilogue titled "The Christian Phenomenon", which openly identified the Omega-Point with God.

However, in an appendix added to the later essay quoted above, Teilhard admitted that it was probably only through a "Revelation" ... "here in its Christian sense", that is to say, "... the beyond making itself manifest 'personally' to the here-below", that the "quasi-negative evidence" presented by humanity's inability to overcome that "death-barrier" can be overcome. Nevertheless, rather than apologize for a faith that appears to attempt to replace what science is telling us, Teilhard believed that he had shown us how there can be a faith that "animates" scientific research. This was apparently because Teilhard, later in life, saw this revelation as providing hope for a future that, despite what he had written years before, science by itself could never guarantee.

We all know, at least if we have lived long enough, how more than in one manner or another, life is like a big lottery. We also know, regardless of whatever meaning or purpose this universe may have, chance or luck has played a major role in its evolution. We've also seen that the chances are this universe itself is going to, one way or another, pass out of existence. And as much as we may desire it, there is probably nothing in our human nature that can *guarantee* our survival after death. Again, in this regard, I want to make it clear that my own view appears to differ somewhat from that of Teilhard, at least as expressed in *The Phenomenon of Man*. However, even if Teilhard's view is understood in a collective sense — that is, that reflective thought will survive — this does not rule out the possibility that at least some individuals, much as is the case in the survival of any species as a whole, will necessarily do so. Nor does this situation rule out the necessity of *grace* (i.e., divine assistance) for its accomplishment. Given all these uncertainties, all we can do, at least as I see it, is to "buy our ticket" by living our lives as best we can, while placing our hopes and our trust in whatever (or Whomever) it is that brought it all to be.

Yet, what does it really mean to live our lives as best we can? This is the second big question — after that of why we have a universe to begin with — that has preoccupied philosophers from almost the very beginning, and the answer all depends on how one sees one's fate. If one sees no purpose or meaning in our existence other than whatever we dream up in our own head, then the old slogan "eat, drink, and be merry (if you can), for tomorrow we die" makes a lot of sense. After all, why bother to care about our neighbor, especially once we get over caring what our neighbor thinks about us? Or even, why bother to care about ourselves? Why not just live quickly and riotously and pack as much as we can into the little time we have left?

On the other hand, if we are willing to bet the meaning of our lives on the possibility that there just might be an eternity awaiting those who prepare themselves for it, then what, in the meantime, will we really have lost? Anything of lasting value? Certainly not, especially if nothing belonging to this world lasts. Fame (even just fifteen minutes worth) or fortune (for at least fifteen years or more) or pleasure — what can any of this mean on a planet, or even universe, in which the ability to support life of any kind may just turn out to be limited? But if there is an eternity, an existence beyond all time, then what is any of these worth against the calculation of oblivion or nothingness?

As we've already seen, there is a real calculus involved. Despite all the incentives, ranging from the more or less selfish, on the one hand, to a genuinely cosmic concern on the other, what we are attempting is a genuine leap of faith, an attempt to break the bonds of our human limitations, and to soar, like astronauts, beyond the boundaries of our terrestrial home. Ventures like this cannot succeed in a climate of passivity and self-doubt. Windows of opportunity come too infrequently to be caught unprepared. Unless we make a firm decision and commitment in the *present*, we will not be ready when the time comes.

Risky? Yes: no doubt it is. It means staking the meaning (and the conduct) of our lives on a goal that transcends purely human concerns and limitations. One could turn out to have been wrong. But suppose one is proven wrong? What truly worthwhile or of really lasting value would we have lost? After all, we could hardly end up being thought fools if there is no one left to do the thinking! Wouldn't we prove to be the much bigger fools if we had the chance to live forever and threw it away?

The reader may have been disappointed to learn that such a world-renowned theologian as Hans Küng does not accept the many gospel stories of the appearances of Jesus after his resurrection as being literally true. Indeed, scripture scholars have long attempted, mostly in vain, to make even much chronological sense of the differing, and seemingly contradictory accounts. All of which, as I pointed out in Chapter 4, leads me to see them, even if taken as literally true, as only being visible or even tangible representations of a state of existence that we cannot comprehend. When the first man to orbit the earth back in 1961, the Soviet "Cosmonaut" Yuri Gagarin, reported that he had looked all around him out in space and had failed to see God or Jesus, I was not the least surprised. Indeed, if he had claimed he had had such a vision, I would have presumed he was hallucinating.

On the other hand, we have seen how, according to Teilhard's view of the very structure of evolution and the improbabilities that, even if only by chance, have been overcome to produce life, the chances are that life is destined in some way to endure, despite whatever happens to the universe. This means that a contemporary theologian like Hans Küng is not acting irrationally when he chooses to believe that death is not the end of everything.

So what can we expect after we die? Maybe Gagarin, who died in a plane crash only seven years after his historic orbit, now knows the answer. But if he is seeing anything, it is not as if he were someone looking at God, as it were, from outside, but rather, in the opinion of the great theologian, Thomas Aquinas, as someone seeing God according to God's essence or being, hence, at least to some extent, sharing in God's own consciousness. Or as Aquinas put it in his massive *Summa Theologica* (I, Q 12, Art. 1&2), as well as in his final summation in his much shorter *Compendium of Theology* (Chap. 106), quoting Psalm 36:9, "…in your [that is, God's] light we see light."

Thus despite all the esoteric symbolism of the Book of Revelation, with its pictures of saints dressed in white robes, strumming harps, or wearing crowns, etc., or the promise, found several times in the Bible, of "a new heaven and a new earth", heaven is not a place or location. It is to enter into, as we said to begin with, *eternity* — which is, by definition, "beyond" or "outside of" either space or time. Thus all the arguments about what a resurrected body would be like, or over who would be married to whom, or over how someone could be possibly happy if someone they loved in this life did not make it into the next, are all so much idle or even irrelevant speculation and, at least to my mind, are probably worth no more than the storied medieval debates over how many angels could dance on the head of pin.

Instead, I would like to take the reader back to one of the earliest Christian theological sayings, or adages, one that has stood the test of time, even though it continues to puzzle many who consider themselves traditional or even conservative Christians. In its shortest and most startling form it is simply this: "God became man that man might become God." The object of this theme, or dream, of *theopoesis* or *theosis* — humans becoming like God — has also been treated from the Jewish perspective by psychologist Eric Fromm, in his book, *You Shall*

Be as Gods, with obvious reference to the Book of Genesis. The specifically Christian expression of this theme dates back to St. Irenaeus (c. 125?-202 CE) and was quickly taken up by succeeding generations of theologians.

To unpack this terse saying, of course, we need to understand "man" as meaning any human being or even all humanity. But even then, how can humans become "God" or even somehow "as if" they merely shared a little bit of divinity? The answer begins with the recognition that only God is by nature immortal or incapable of dying. So if God took on human nature so that God could experience death, which is what Christians believe God did in the case of Jesus, then it becomes possible for humans, in turn, to share in God's immortality. Thus, the logic of this exchange is that once God took this step, God allows us to share divine nature and that by sharing this life, we can become, even if only in the slightest degree, but still, in a very real sense, like God. Or as the Second Epistle of Peter (1:4) says, we become "sharers in the divine nature." Or, still again, as Jesus is portrayed as saying in the Gospel of John (10:10), "I have come to bring life that you may have it more abundantly."

Yet, is any of this believable? I suppose that the answer to this question is whether or not we believe in God to begin with. For those who do believe, then almost anything is possible, at least providing that God wills it. And for those who do not believe, the idea that we could possibly live a new life after we have died would certainly seem far-fetched or highly unlikely.

In fact, we have already noted how Pascal tried to calculate the probability of this happening. Many have criticized his argument as being self-serving. Perhaps so: it seems that just short of eight years before his death, he underwent a kind of mystical or "peak experience" in which the presence of God was so palpable that he wrote an extended note or record of what had happened and sewed it into the lining of his vest. The note was discovered only after his death. This experience marked what he called his "second conversion" and caused him to largely leave mathematics and scientific experiments behind and to turn instead to devote the rest of his short life — he died at age 39 — to philosophy and theology. Thus, it could be that his famous "wager" may have been mostly his own attempt to persuade himself that what he had already experienced was not some kind of self-induced hallucination.

If so, then perhaps we may learn something, and that is that faith and doubt are not so much opposites as they are simply two sides of the same phenomenon. If our beliefs were about absolute certainties, would there be any room for real faith? I very much doubt it. Our puny minds can only grasp so much. It has taken millions of years of evolution for our primate ancestors to even reach the point of self-awareness, not just to be able to know, but "to know that we know" and thus wonder about our own existence. So should we be surprised that we cannot conceive exactly just what a life after death might be like or that our powers of reasoning can only, at the most, tell us only what it must not be? Thus, the Book of Revelation (21:4), despite all its lavish attempts to tell us what heaven will be like, probably comes closest when it says that

> Death will be no more; mourning and crying and pain will be no more, for the first things have passed away...

So how, or perhaps just as important, *when* shall we decide? Can a decision about something this vital to our future — presupposing that there is a chance of such a future — be postponed indefinitely? I suppose it can be, but only to our detriment. Instead, I will take up Pascal's challenge, aided by Teilhard's recalculation of the odds, and repeat the other quote (Rev 22:5) that Hans Küng used in closing his book on *The Beginning of All Things*, a book which he began by quoting the "Let there be light" of Genesis 1:3. Thus, in view of what we now know about the explosion of energy that marked the beginning of the universe, we can envision of how it might all end for those who choose wisely:

> And there will be no more night; and they need no lamp or sun, for the Lord God will be their light, and they will reign forever and ever.

Some Final Thoughts

After all is said and done, I think that the case for eternal life, as I have presented it in this book, comes down to what Plato had to say in *Timaeus* about "the good" being diffusive of itself and turning it into an ontological statement, that is, concerning *being* itself. Thus, whether we choose, as did Plato, to personify that *good* as "God" or simply leave it as an abstract value or principle, the assumption is that it is better to be than not to be. Otherwise, it seems to me to be impossible to explain why anyone would dream of a life beyond death, or why, knowing what we now know about the origin and probable death of the universe, theorists have dreamt up their dreams of multiple universes or of a "multiverse" without end.

I realize that many people cannot bring themselves to accept such a revelation or to have such a faith in the future, even if they wish they could. Freud and the self-designated "New Atheists" have made it almost impossible for many to hope for or accept the promise of eternal life, at least without fearing they are only giving in to wishful thinking or outright deluding themselves.

Even Jung's testimony—quoted at the beginning of Chapter 6 — about the need to recover a religious outlook on life might lead one to think that humanity in general is more psychologically needier than we'd like to admit.

Forever

However, I think that I may have come across a method of bridging this divide without taking any unreasonable leap of faith. It came to me some years ago when I first began to realize that I too have to face the fact that I might only have a few more years left to live. And it was also partly motivated by my admiration for the concise summary of Christ's teaching by the unknown author claiming the name "Barnabas" quoted at the beginning of Chapter 3 of this book.

As I saw it then, and as I still see it now, there are *three* basic "facts of life" plus an optional "Christian corollary" which I believe offers the best and most realistic way of dealing with those three facts.

First, we have the *physical* fact that nothing in this life, whether it be our accomplishments, or most likely, even the universe itself, will survive forever. Sooner or later everything appears destined to come to an end.

Second, we have the *psychological* fact that few or even none of us are really comfortable with the first fact. In fact, we do everything possible to blot it out of our minds, or failing that, inure or insulate ourselves against it. Thus, in addition to the speculations about other "universes", we have our own natural tendency to place our hopes in what I call "the three Fs"— family, fortune, and fame — as if any of these could guarantee some form of immortality, which, in the end, they cannot.

Some Final Thoughts

Third, there is the *spiritual* fact that all the great religions have taught that the only effective way of dealing with both of the first two facts is to, one way or another, divest ourselves of our ego-centricity and learn to fix our minds upon and to live for the sake of something or some cause or purpose greater than ourselves.

Of course, I realize that there can be many such causes or purposes, and that not all of them are all that worthwhile or even worthy of our commitment. History is littered with the ruins of them, or even the corpses of those foolishly gave their lives or were the victims of such causes, including overtly religious ones.

However, this is where the specifically Christian option comes in. And oddly enough, it came most forcefully to me from the insight of an agnostic of Jewish ancestry, — the same Ernest Becker whose Pulitzer Prize-winning book, *The Denial of Death,* I mentioned in the third chapter. According to Becker, while almost all religions in history have attempted to either deny death or to escape it altogether, Christianity is the religion that has most strongly emphasized that the only way to cope with death is to *go through it willingly* — even if reluctantly — as the only way to pass *beyond* it.

No doubt some, perhaps many, will say that this is an exaggerated claim, even if Dietrich Bonhöffer, the Evangelical Lutheran theologian who was executed by the Nazis in 1945 for his part in a plot to kill Adolph Hitler, had made much the same claim. Bonhöffer, in fact, seems to have insisted that Christianity should not even be considered a "religion" at all, at least in the usual sense, based on his judgment that most religions have functioned more or less as escape hatches from reality.

In any case, even if we forget what Becker or Bonhöffer wrote — or counter with examples such as both the ancient Egyptian "Book of the Dead" detailing what might await us in the next world, or its more recent Tibetan counterpart, focusing on the process of dying, — ask yourself what other of the world's religions has the cross, no matter how abstractly rendered, or even the crucifix, with the image of a dying person or corpse nailed to it, as its central symbol or even object of devotion? Can you imagine any other religion doing this, let's say with its hero or object of faith depicted hanging at the end of a noose (as happened to Bonhöffer) or strapped to an electric chair?

Or again, as the celebrated fourth century Syrian poet St. Ephrem the Deacon once put it:

> Death trampled our Lord [Christ] underfoot, but he in his turn treated death as a highroad for his own feet...It [death] was able to kill natural human life, but was itself killed by the life that is above the nature of man.
>
> (*Sermo de Domino Nostro*, 4)

However, even if one does not accept all the traditional Christian doctrines, such as those found in the Nicene Creed where Jesus is declared not just "Son of God" in the metaphorical or biblical sense but literally "God from true God" and "consubstantial with"— that is, of the same nature as "the Father" or almighty God, — one can still follow in the footsteps of Jesus. This can be done by living or following, as best one can, the example of Jesus or as did Albert Schweitzer, the theologian turned medical missionary, or Dag Hammarskjöld, the second Executive Secretary of the United Nations, who died in an airplane crash during his effort to bring peace in the Congo. Each followed, in his own way, *The Imitation of Christ,* — in fact, a copy of this medieval spiritual classic was found in Hammarskjöld's luggage. In other words, we should be asking ourselves "What would Jesus do" and doing our best to do the same.

Seen from this perspective, that of Jesus, I'm not at all surprised or scandalized to meet Christians who nevertheless doubt or even sometimes even feel, like Jesus did on the cross, that God has abandoned them. Nor am I upset by the fact that while many think of Christianity as "ascensional",— that is, primarily a way "up" to heaven — others consider that their spirituality, even if they are not formally Christians, must be more expansive or even "horizontal", to be lived more in reaching out, like the arms of the cross, to embrace the needs of the whole world.

Regardless of whichever path is chosen, however, I think it is necessary to stress yet again that religion or spirituality must take us *beyond* ourselves and our own selfish concerns. It is only in forgetting or "losing" ourselves that we shall find salvation, or as the Buddha taught, it is only through *anatta* or selflessness that we will reach *nirvana*.

This is why we find repeated warnings by spiritual teachers against false mysticisms that promise short-cuts to ecstasy or that we find in the gospels warnings against attitudes of pious self-righteousness. Above all, the hope for eternal life or for "heaven" is a hope for *transcendence,* which means, first of all, transcendence from or beyond self. From a purely logical standpoint, if there would be anything blocking the possibility of eternal life, if there is such a possibility, it would not be lack of firm belief, but a lack of the *desire* to have anything more than this life or the rejection of anything or anyone better than ourselves, or the refusal to take the *risk* that faith demands, which is to be able to pass beyond the self-concerned need for absolute certainty. Thus, as Jesus might say, and indeed did say a number of times about those who prided themselves on being superior or already having it all now, "Truly I say to you, they have received their reward."

No doubt this is a hard saying. Yet I think that it remains a fact of life, as well as a hard fact of evolution. Thus, Teilhard, dealing with the problem of evil as we experience it in this world, wrote in the very last sentence of the appendix that he added to *The Phenomenon of Man,* that, in light of our evolutionary origins as well as both the advances as well as setbacks of history, "In one manner or the other it still remains true that, even in the view of a mere biologist, the human epic resembles nothing so much as a way of the Cross."

That "way of the Cross" is, of course, an allusion to the once popular Lenten devotion imported from the Holy Land tracing out the steps of Jesus to his execution. It began with a meditation of his condemnation by Pilate and his being scourged and mocked by the Roman soldiers, followed by the imposition of the cross on his shoulders and his stumbling and falls beneath its weight, followed by his crucifixion, death, and burial. All this Teilhard likened to the evolution of human life in the face of suffering.

Yet, may not the same be said on a larger scale regarding life in all its forms on this earth, its continual suppression and apparent failure only to keep rising again to continue the struggle, even if only to what appears to be its final defeat and disappearance?

So too in our own lives lived through the initial stages of growth and struggle to the flourishing of our prime, then, most often, through the slow but certain decline into old age, infirmity, and, in the end, to our graves — all this despite whatever plans and hopes we may have had for the future. In the face of this truth we all live, each in our own way, as Thoreau wrote, "lives of quiet desperation".

Forever

What then keeps us going? For many, it is the distractions, the diversions, even the oblivion afforded by living. For many others, however, it is the hope of and the quest for something else, for a life, however ill-defined and nebulous it may seem, beyond this present one. So too, I believe, it was for Jesus himself and who, against all odds, persisted in his course to its consummation when in the end he handed over what was left of his life to divine providence — the God whom he called "Father".

Perhaps there really wasn't anything new in this old story. In one guise or another, humankind has probably always dreamed of or hoped for something beyond this life. And perhaps this hope is, as the skeptics insist, nothing but the "tales told by nursemaids". If so, then we are all, — and here I speak of humanity in general, — more foolish than we may have hitherto imagined.

However, given the alternative, which is the end of evolution and of all that lives, not just on this planet, but eventually elsewhere in this vast universe, such an outcome, as I stated earlier, I can't even imagine.

But in the year or so that has separated the first edition of this book from this latest edition, I have begun to think of life, especially eternal life, more in specifically theological terms; that is to say, not just in terms of individual immortality, but in relation to what might be called the future of God. I may have insisted, like Augustine and Aquinas, on the difference between God as *Being,* — or like Tillich or Eckhart long before him, who described God as the "Ground" of all being, — and our own *existence* as mere creatures.

As of late, I have begun to realize that our continued existence, whether as individuals or as species, can only be guaranteed by our relationship to, or more exactly, our union with a God who is not understood simply as *Being* as such or in itself, but as still in the process of *Becoming,* — a process, which Teilhard, borrowing from the vocabulary of the Epistles to the Ephesians and Colossians, described as "pleromisation". Or as he once confided to a friend, the "Pleroma" is not just a completion of the universe, but is also "in some sense a 'completion' of God."

This would be, without doubt, a radical revision in our thinking about God, who has been traditionally seen as essentially complete and self-sufficient, and in no way obliged to create a universe except through the impulse of pure love. However, this line of thought would almost necessarily lead us into the thought of Teilhard's contemporary, the philosopher Alfred North Whitehead, who wrote rather densely about both the "antecedent" and the "consequent" natures of God in the concluding section of his huge treatise *Process and Reality* — a subject that I have postponed dealing with until my next book.

However, there is one aspect of Whitehead's thought that is particularly of interest in respect to what I have written in this book. This is the debate

Forever

among Whitehead's disciples, especially those who call themselves "Process Theologians", as to whether the individual immortality that Whitehead spoke of is truly *subjective* in the literal sense, implying a continuation of our state of consciousness as individual subjects. Or is it more strictly *objective*, for example, passing on our thoughts in our writings, our strokes of genius expressed in works of art, or simply in passing our genes to the next generation, or maybe our fortune (if we had one) to our heirs, or our reputation, whether it be for good or ill.

Many, of course, think or say they would be content with the latter, especially if it turns out to beneficial to those who follow us. But all talk of "objective immortality" this assumes, as Whitehead seemed to, that the whole evolutionary "process" that he talked and wrote about would go on forever, an assumption that contemporary cosmology — at least that based observational science and not simply imaginative speculation — has very much left in doubt. If so, then we are taken back to the overall thesis of this book and if that is the case, and evolution, and everything it has produced, is destined to eventually end in virtual nothingness, then that is not a conclusion that I am yet prepared to accept. As I have said before, I have bet or waged my whole life on this not being the case.

Richard W. Kropf
April 20, 2017

Appendix A

A Note on Christian Universalism and Conditional Immortality

In this note, we will attempt, as briefly as possible, to review two suggested alternatives to the customary Christian viewpoint that after death that, aside from the Catholic view that a soul might be detained temporarily in "Purgatory" before being admitted to heaven, that ultimately the soul faces either of two fates, either heaven or hell, and that both will last for all eternity.

The first and oldest alternative view is that known as "Universalism", the belief that everyone, at least in the end, will be admitted to heaven or the state of eternal beatitude. Most famously known for this belief was the early Christian scripture scholar and theologian, Origen of Alexandria (c.185-254), although a similar opinion was held also by his mentor, St. Clement, bishop of Alexandria. It was a view that was also held by St. Gregory of Nyssa (d. 395) and quite a few other notable early church theologians well into the fifth century until Emperor Justinian (483-565), prevailed upon the bishops of his time to have many of Origen's views condemned and suppressed at the Second Council of Constantinople in 553. Although it still remains a matter of debate as to what extent Origen's universalism was explicitly condemned, it may be surmised that Justinian, most famous for his codification of Roman law, feared that, without the threat of an eternity of punishment to back up the moral code, the stability of civil society would be threatened.

However, the idea of universal forgiveness never completely died out, even in the West, where in the ninth century the Irish scholar and philosopher, John Scotus Eriugena, revived it on the basis of his readings of Gregory of Nyssa. And since then, it has been again revived by Unitarians and other "universalists" (see especially Robert Wild's survey of the subject as listed in the Bibliography).

The arguments in favor of this point of view are not all that complex. The first, already mentioned in this book, is simply the goodness of God. How could an infinitely good God supposedly condemn finite or limited beings like ourselves to an infinite or eternal state of torture, no matter how bad we may have been?

Add to this the fact that scripture attests in a number of places that God wishes everyone to be saved (e.g., 1 Tim 2:4) and even that it is God's intention to "restore" (*apokatastaseōs*) all creation to its original condition (Acts 3:21), hence Origen's use of the tongue-twisting word *apokatastasis* to sum up this concept of universal restoration of everything, including the fallen angels, to their original spiritual

Appendix A

state. However, this universal restoration, in Origen's estimation, was not really the end of the world, but rather the end of this phase or era of God's creative activity, only one of many successive creations to follow! (See Quasten, Vol. II, p. 89-90.)

All this brings up what is meant by eternity and such terms as "eternal life" or "eternal punishment". As was pointed out on page 26 of this book, for something to be *eternal* means that it is literally *without* or *outside of time*, and thus strictly speaking, only God, whose being, in a sense "predates" creation, can be truly eternal. Accordingly, some very astute scholars have pointed that in the original Greek of the New Testament only God is described as being eternal or *aidios* (as in Rom 1:20), while everything else that lasts "forever" is described by the adjective *aiōnios* and the noun *aiōnas* — words that imply the passage of time, as in the phrase *aiōnas tōn aiōnōn*, found in Revelations 11:15, describing Christ's reign, and translated in the NRSV as meaning "forever and ever". Thus, according to St. Paul (1 Cor 15: 26-28), it will only be at the very end of time, when death itself has been destroyed, that this dominion of Christ will be "subjected" to God, or that the final point is reached wherein "God becomes all in all."

Consequently, these same scholars point out that the translation of the Greek adjective *aiōnios* into the Latin *aeternus* as found in St. Augustine's writings and in Jerome's Latin translation of the Bible are unfortunately mistranslations, especially unfortunate because they have led to the idea that once "sent" to hell from which no one, regardless how severely chastened or repentant, shall ever emerge, a view that has probably have led to countless rebellions against God and religion in general.

Perhaps, Augustine, a North African of Roman descent, who confessed that he detested Greek when forced to study it as a schoolboy, can be forgiven. But Jerome, who was very familiar with Greek as well, and even tried to learn Hebrew to better translate the Bible (the traditional Latin "Vulgate" translation), perhaps can't be so easily excused, nor can the translators of the NRSV and other supposedly up-to-date biblical translations. In any case, the results of these mistranslations have been unfortunate, not simply in terms of the fear-driven preaching of hellfire and brimstone that has plagued Christianity since the Middle Ages, but even more in the predestinarian theology and the pessimism among the unfortunate, as well as the arrogance among the fortunate, who thereby considered themselves among the "saved", that it has spawned.

However, I think that this whole problem and the belief in universalism, at least as far as it came about, especially as a counterweight to the grim threat of eternal damnation, to a large extent also has to be understood in the context of the Platonism, and the philosophical dualism that characterized it, that

Appendix A

prevailed in the largely Greek-speaking world of early Christianity. For a Christian Platonist, like Origen, the human soul was seen as naturally immortal, having a spiritual existence even before it entered the material world, and as such, destined to outlive, whether we like or not, life in our bodies. Hence the problem of what becomes of the souls of those who have lived in a state of complete opposition to God. Are they to be tormented for ever and ever or even for eternity, as Augustine saw it, wishing to die but unable to? Or are they to be given a reprieve or a second chance — in effect turning an everlasting hell into a more temporary purgatory?

Every theology, understood as an attempt to explain ones beliefs, to a large extent depends on an underlying philosophical system, which in turn is generally dependent on a cosmology or overall world-view. The cosmology presented in the opening chapters of this book is one that is very different than that assumed by Origen, Augustine and all the early Church scholars and even most theologians up until recent times. This new approach is based on an evolutionary science that encompasses everything from the beginning to the end, from the initial "Big Bang" until the last breath of life takes place in the farthest reaches of the universe.

Within this evolutionary vision, I too would very much like to believe that every human mind or "soul", or that of whatever other intelligent life there may exist elsewhere in a still-expanding the universe, is very much capable, at least with God's help, of eventually evolving into a spirit capable of living in union with God not just "forever", but even beyond the boundaries of time, or at least beyond that point where total entropy (as described in Chapter 2) takes place and the universe suffers what has been paradoxically called a total "heat-death" and even hell — if there really is such a place — literally freezes over.

However, the main problem with the universalist view is that, no matter how venerable and well-intentioned as it may be, it nevertheless seems to undercut the freedom of the human will and, with it, the power to definitively choose either for or against God, and in doing so, blunting the existential message of the Gospel.

For this reason, there has appeared in more recent times an alternative view or, to be more accurate, two closely-related views, one known, in rather menacing terms, as "Annihilationism", and the other, focusing more on individual responsibility, known as "Conditional Immortality". (Both of these views have also been recently explored by Robert Wild in an addition volume as listed in the Bibliography.) While both of these views envision the ultimate disappearance of the unsaved or unredeemed, the first would seem to be predicated on the Platonic assumption of the natural immortality of the human soul, thus leaving the impression that God is left with the rather vengeful task of eliminating the existence of a recalcitrant soul that would otherwise live forever.

In contrast to annihilationism, the "conditional" aspect of the alternative version is based on an altogether different view of human nature. It holds that just as in the course of biological evolution, not only individuals, but even whole species, have disappeared, it perhaps seems a bit presumptuous to suppose that human beings are somehow an exception. It is for this reason that the possibility of immortality is seen as depending entirely on a person's cooperation with God's help or God's grace. Thus there is no question of God "annihilating" a soul that would otherwise exist but simply a matter of God allowing a person who could have chosen to taken up God's offer but has chosen to do otherwise, to simply pass out of existence.

Nevertheless — perhaps that it is here where faith alone can intervene and give us hope — that in the end not only death itself will be defeated, but that *everyone* of us among the living or the dead who have ever lived, regardless as to how mistaken or even sinful we may have been, will somehow become swept up in that great *plērōma* ("fullness" or "completion") envisioned by Paul or his earliest disciples in the epistles to the Ephesians (1:10,29; 3;19; 4:13) and to the Colossians (1:19; 2:9-10) and by one his most recent disciples, the visionary Jesuit

Forever

priest and paleontologist, Pierre Teilhard de Chardin. If so, then perhaps it is only this point when time itself has been completed, that "forever", no matter how long it way have actually lasted, truly passes into "eternity". Should that turn out to be the case, then even "everlasting" punishment would turn out to have been, at the very most, even if it lasted until the end of time, still only temporary.

Appendix B

Karl Rahner's Final Vision of Eternity

Below is the conclusion of an address given by theologian Karl Rahner at his 80th birthday celebration, held on February 11-12, 1984, about six weeks before his death. I am indebted to Rudolf Goetz, MD, for this translation made from a tape recording of Rahner's speech and supplemented with the help of a translation of the text of the whole address that appeared in *Theological Studies,* No. 61, 2000.

If we Christians profess the eternal life we hope to partake in, then this expectation of the coming is nothing strange. Usually, one speaks with a certain unctuous pathos about the hope of eternal life; and far be it from me to find fault in that, as long as it is meant genuinely. Yet, I am touched strangely if I hear such a talk. It seems to me that the schemes of imagination, seeking clarification of the eternal life, fit very little to the radical incision that death actually is. The eternal life is so tellingly called "on the other side", and as continuing "after" death. One imagines that eternal life too much equipped with the realities that are familiar for us here: as joy and peace, as festival meal and jubilation; and all that, and similar, never ending and continuing on and on. I am afraid that the radical incomprehensibility of what is really meant by eternal life is made harmless; what we, in this life, call the immediate vision of God is degraded to one pleasurable occupation among others that fill that eternal life. The ineffable enormity is not truly perceived; that the absolute God-head Itself, naked and bare, breaks into our narrow "creatureliness". I confess that it seems to me to be an agonizing, not yet mastered, task for a theologian of today to discover a better imaginative model for this, one that would exclude, a priori, these ineffective ones just described. But how, but how?

Once the angels of death have cleaned out from the spaces of our mind all that insignificant rubble that we call our human history—even though, of course, the true essence of freedom remains; once all the glowing stars of our ideals (that we used, in our pride, to drape the sky of our existence) have faded away in their glow, and are extinguished; once death has erected a huge silent emptiness, and once we have accepted this silently, in faith and hope, as our genuine essence, then our past life (even as long as it may be) appears only as a short explosion of our freedom that had seemed to us stretched out like in slow motion, an explosion in which question turns into answer, possibility into reality, time into eternity, freedom offered into freedom done. And once it becomes apparent that the gigantic shock that we sense as death [will become] ineffable jubilation, that this gigantic silent emptiness, is, in truth, full of the central basic mystery that we call God, full of His pure light, of His love that takes and gives everything, then [perhaps], out of this mystery, also the countenance of Jesus, the blessed one, appears and looks at us. It is in this concreteness [of Christ] that we have a divine surpassing of all our usual ideas regarding the incomprehensibility of the infinite God.

I don't want, really, to describe vaguely, what comes, but rather, still hint at, with stammering, how one can expect, preliminarily, this *coming*, by experiencing the sinking in death, as the rising of that what comes. Eighty years are a long time. For every person, however, the allotted lifetime is the short moment in which becomes what has to be.

And now, very honorable audience—I don't want to speak again after the celebration—I thank you already now, very cordially, for your participation in this little history… that is [?] an 80th birthday. I thank you from my heart and ask you that I may be dispensed from rhetorically elaborating on this "thank you". I thank you, cordially, and ask you, as an ordinary Christian …who knows what is important, possibly to carry once a small prayer before God that His love and His mercy may be my part in finality.

Karl Rahner, S.J., born on March 5, 1904 in Freiburg, Germany, died in Innsbruck, Austria, on March 30, 1984. Highly influential at the Second Vatican Council, he is often considered to have been one of the greatest Catholic theologians of the 20th century.

Bibliography

Alter, Robert. *The Book of Psalms,* New York: W. W. Norton, 2007.

Aquinas, Thomas. *Compendium Theologiae.* Translated by Cyril Vollert, S.J., St. Louis & London: B. Herder Books, 1947.
————— *Summa Theologica.* Translation by the English Dominican Province. Electronic edition, Claremont, CA: Coyote Canyon Press, 2011.

Aristotle. *Aristotle's Collection* (29 Books). Amazon Kindle Books.

Alexander, Eben. *Proof of Heaven: A Neurosurgeon's Journey into the Afterlife.* New York: Simon Schuster, 2012.

Audouze, Jean & Israël, Guy, editors. *Cambridge Atlas of Astronomy,* New York: Cambridge University Press, 1988.

Augustine, St. *Confessions.* Transl. by Vernon J. Bourke. New York: Cima Publishing Co., 1953.

Baird, Robert D. & Bloom, Alfred, in *Indian and Far Eastern Religious Traditions.* New York: Harper & Row, 1971.

Barrow, John D. *The Origin of the Universe.* New York: HarperCollins–Basic Books, 1994.
————— and Tipler, Frank J., *The Cosmological Anthropic Principle.* New York: Oxford University Press, 1988.

Becker, Ernest. *The Denial of Death.* New York: Macmillan, 1973.

Bibliography

Bergson, Henri. *Creative Evolution.* Translated by Arthur Mitchell, Ph.D. New York: Henry Holt & Co., 1911. (Amazon Kindle edition)
———— *The Two Sources of Morality and Religion.* Notre Dame , IN: University of Notre Dame Press, 1977.

Blondel, Maurice. *Action: Essay on a Critique of Life and a Science of Practice.* Notre Dame, IN: University of Notre Dame Press, 1984.

Chaisson, Eric J. *Cosmic Evolution: The Rise of Complexity in Nature.* Cambridge, MA: Harvard University Press, 2001.

Cobb, John B. & Ives, Christopher. *The Emptying God: A Buddhist-Jewish-Christian Conversation.* Maryknoll, NY: Orbis Books, 1990.

Darwin, Charles. *Autobiography.* Edited by Francis Darwin. Amazon Kindle Edition.
———— *On the Origin of Species.* New York: Random House, 1979.
———— *The Descent of Man.* A Public Domain Book. Amazon Kindle Edition.

De Lubac, Henri. *The Mystery of the Supernatural.* Translated by Rosemary Sheed, Montreal: Palm Publishers, 1947.

Dudek, John F. *Consciousness and the Material Soul: A Consensus of Religion and Science.* Notre Dame, IN: Cross Cultural Publications, 2001.

Fowler, James W. *The Stages of Faith: The Psychology of Human Development and the Quest for Meaning,* New York: Harper & Row, 1980.
———— *Becoming Adult: Becoming Christian.* Harper & Row, 1984.

Forever

Frankl, Viktor. *Man's Search for Meaning: An Introduction to Logotherapy.* New York: Pocket Books, 1959, 1963.
——— *The Will to Meaning: Foundations and Applications of Logotherapy.* New York: New American Library, 1969.
——— *The Unconscious God: Psychotherapy and Theology.* New York: Simon & Schuster, 1979.

Freud, Sigmund. *Civilization and Its Discontents.* Translated by David McLintock. New York: Penguin Books, 2002.
——— *The Future of an Illusion.* Translated by W. D. Robson-Scott. Mansfield Centre, CT: Martino Publishing, 2011.

Fromm, Eric. *You Shall Be As Gods: A Radical Interpretation of the Old Testament and Its Tradition.* New York: Holt, Rinehart and Winston, 1966.

Glimm, Francis X., translator. "The Letter of Barnabas", *The Apostolic Fathers.* New York: Cima Publishing Co., 1947.

Goudge, T. A. *The Ascent of Life: A Philosophical Study of the Theory of Evolution.* Toronto: University of Toronto Press, 1961

Hawking, Stephen & Mlodinow, Leonard. *The Grand Design.* New York: Bantam Books, 2010.

Isaacson, Walter. *Einstein: His Life and Universe.* New York: Simon & Schuster, 2007

John of the Cross, St. *The Collected Works of St. John of the Cross.* Translated by Kieran Kavanaugh, O.C.D. and Otilio Rodriguez, O.C.D. Washington, DC: Institute for Carmelite Studies, 1964, 1973.

Bibliography

Jung, Carl Gustav. *Modern Man in Search of a Soul.* English translation London: Kegan Paul Trench Kubner, 1933.

Kaufmann. Walter. *Critique of Religion and Philosophy.* New York: Harper & Row, 1958.
———— *The Faith of a Heretic.* New York: Doubleday, 1963.

Kant, Immanuel. *A Critque of Pure Reason.* Translation by J. M. D. Meiklejohn, A Public Domain Book, 2011.

Kitigawa, Joseph M. *Religions of the East.* Philadelphia: Westminster Press, 1974.

Kropf, Richard W. *Faith, Security and Risk: The Dynamics of Spiritual Growth,* Mahwah, NJ: Paulist Press, 1990, and Eugene OR: Wipf & Stock Publishers, 2005.

Küng, Hans. *Eternal Life? Life After Death as a Medical, Philosophical, and Theological Problem.* Garden City, NY: Doubleday, 1985.
———— *The Beginning of All Things: Science and Religion.* Translated by John Bowden. Grand Rapids , MI: Wm. B. Eerdmans Publishing, 2007

Lakoff, George, & Johnson, Mark. *Philosophy in the Flesh: The Embodied Mind and Its Challenge to Western Thought.* New York: Basic Books, 1999.

Maslow, Abraham H. *Religions, Values, and Peak Experiences.* New York: Viking Books, 1970.

McKenzie, John L., "Aspects of Old Testament Thought" in *The Jerome Biblical Commentary.* Brown, Fitzmyer, and Murphy, editors. Engelwood, NJ: Prentice Hall, 1968.

Meier, John P. *A Marginal Jew: Rethinking the Historical Jesus.* Vol. III. New York: Doubleday, 2001

Moody, Raymond A. *The Light Beyond.* New York: Bantam Books, 1988.

North, Robert, S.J. *Teilhard and the Creation of the Soul.* Milwaukee: Bruce Publishing Co., 1968.

Pascal, Blaise. *Pensées.* Introduction by T. S. Eliot. New York: E. P. Dutton,1958.

Plato, "The Apology", *The Complete Works of Plato.* Translation by Benjamin Jowett. Oxford: The Complete Works Collection, 2011.

Provenzano, Joseph P. *The Philosophy of Conscious Energy.* Nashville, TN: Winston-Derek, 1993; republished as *Conscious Energy*, Lincoln, NE: iUniverse, 2000.
———— & Kropf, Richard W. *Logical Faith: Introducing a Scientific Approach to Spirituality and Religion.* Bloomington IN: iUniverse, 2009.

Puligandla, R. *Fundamentals of Indian Philosophy.* Nashville, TN: Abington Press, 1975.

Quasten, Johannes. *Patrology: Vol II, Ante-Nicene Literature after Irenaeus.* Westminster, MD: Newman/Spectrum, 1953.

Rahner, Karl. *Hominisation: The Evolutionary Origin of Man as a Theological Problem*, translated by W.T. O'Hara. New York: Herder and Herder, 1966.
———— *Encyclopedia of Theology: The Concise* Sacramentum Mundi, ed. New York, Seabury Press, 1975

Bibliography

———— *The Foundations of Theology: An Introduction to the Idea of Christianity*. Translated by William V. Dych. New York: Seabury Press, 1978.

Randall, Lisa. *Knocking on Heaven's Door: How Physics and Scientific Thinking Illuminate the Universe and the Modern World.* New York: HarperCollins, 2011.

Rees, Martin. *A Scientist's Warning: How Terror, Error, and Environmental Disaster Threaten Humankind's Future in This Century — on Earth and Beyond.* New York: Basic Books, 2003.

Robinson, James M. editor. *The Nag Hammadi Library*, San Francisco: Harper & Row, 1988.

Russell, Robert J., Stoeger, William R., and Coyne, George V., eds. *Physics, Philosophy, and Theology: A Common Quest for Understanding.* Vatican Observatory/Notre Dame University Press, 1988.

Sagan, Carl. *Cosmos*. New York: Random House, 1980.

Smith, Wilfred Cantwell. *Faith and Belief.* Princeton University Press, 1970.

Spong, John Shelby. *Eternal Life: A New Vision: Beyond Religion, Beyond Theism, Beyond Heaven and Hell.* San Francisco: HarperOne, 2010.

Taylor, Charles. *A Secular Age*. Harvard University Press, 2007.

The Teachings of the Second Vatican Council. Introduction by Gregory Baum. Westminster, MD: Newman Press, 1966.

Forever

Teilhard de Chardin, Pierre. *The Phenomenon of Man.* Intro. by Julian Huxley. London: Wm. Collins Sons & Co.; New York: Harper & Brothers, 1959.

———— *The Divine Milieu.* London: Wm. Collins Sons & Co; New York: Harper & Brothers, 1960.

———— *Letters from a Traveler.* London: Wm. Collins Sons & Co.: New York: Harper & Brothers, 1962.

———— *The Future of Man.* New York: Harper & Row, 1964.

———— *Human Energy.* London: Collins, 1969.

———— *The Activation of Energy.* London: Collins, 1970.

———— *Christianity and Evolution.* New York: Harcourt Brace Jovanovich, 1971.

———— *The Heart of Matter.* New York: Harcourt Brace, 1978.

Tipler, Frank W. *The Physics of Immortality: Modern Physics, God, and the Resurrection of the Dead.* New York: Doubleday, 1988.

Wild, Robert. *A Catholic Reading Guide to Universalism.* Eugene, OR: Wipf & Stock Publishers, 2015.

———— *A Catholic Reading Guide to Conditional Immortality.* Eugene, OR: Wipf & Stock Publishers, 2017.

Index

Note: In this index the names and terms beginning with an upper case letter refer to primary topics. Subtopics (except when referring to proper names) begin in lower case.

Agnostics, salvation of, p. 71
Aquinas, Thomas, p. 48, 66, 112, 138
Alexander, Eben, p. 79, 81, 138
Anatta, p. 58, 121
Animism, p. 44
Anthropic Principle, p. 91, 138
Aristotle, p. 45, 48, 92, 138
Atman, p. 50
Atheism, Atheists, p. 33, "new"-, p. 117; salvation of, p. 71
Augustine, St., p. 8, 17, 26, 66, 90, 138
Baptism, p. 69-71
Barnabas, epistle of, p.31, 118, 140
Bashar, p. 45, 60
Becker, Ernest, p. 13, 119, 138
Being and existence, p. 66
Belief(s): relationship to faith, p. 64, 71-72, 115, 143; philosophical, p.44, p. 60; scientific, p. 19, 29, 40, 100
Bergson, Henri, p. 14, 19-20, 39, 41, 75, 100, 104-105, 139
Bible: on human nature, p. 45-47; comparison with Buddhist views, p. 58-59; St. Paul's translation of biblical view, p. 60
Big Bang, p. 2-3, 41, 101; repeated? p. 25, 57
Blondel, Maurice, p. 102-103, 139
Boethius, p. 26
Bonhöffer, Dietrich, p. 119-120
Brahman, p. 50
Buddha (See Gautama)
Buddhism, p. 58-59
Chaisson, Eric, p. 26-27, 139
Change; evolutionary, p. 61; and illusion, p. 50; of mind, p. 78
Charity (see Love)

Christ: imitation of, p. 121; as pinnacle of evolution, p. 102; resurrection of, p. 32, 109; spirit of, p. 59 ; as symbol of God, p. 108; universal, p. 98; victory of, p. 120

Christianity: attraction of, p. 37; as "religion", p. 121

Church: censorship by, p. 97, 101; constitution, 96; definition of, 70; failure of, p. 76; membership in, 55, 70-71

Consciousness: co-consciousness, p. 102; of death, p. 22, 53; divine, p. 112 ; field of, p. 52; self-, p. 35 , 57; and soul, p. 136

Contemplation, p. 79

Conversion, of ancient world, p. 37, as internal, 70; sudden, p.74; second, p. 115

Co-reflection, p. 108-109

Cross: symbol of, p. 122-123

Crusades, p. 34

Cryonics, p. 16, 48

Dante, p. 37

Dark Energy & Matter, p. 25

Darwin, Charles, p. 7, 11, 39, 128; centennial, p. 18, 102-103

Dead, Book of the (Egyptian & Tibetan), p. 120

Dead Sea Scrolls, p. 46

Death: -barrier, p.107, 109; brain death, p. 87; denial of, p. 13, 135; elimination of, p.13; fear of, p. 22, 53; Freud on, p.67; life after, p. 43-44, 60; meaning of, p. 22; premature, p. 74; Socrates on, p. 36; sudden, p. 43; triumph over, p. 120; of universe, p. 24-25: also see Near-death experiences

De Lubac, Henri, p. 94, 139

Delusion, p. 80

Descartes, Rene, p. 57

Devil, (see Satan)

Dogma, dogmatism, p. 71-72

Earth (planet): evolution of life on, p. 99, 123; future of, p.14, 23; kingdom of God on, 70

Eccelesiastes, book of, p. 46

Index

Einstein, Albert: cosmological constant and relativity, p. 25, 40; on energy, p. 52; on fear of death, p. 15, 53; on space-time, p. 26

Élan vital, p. 14, 39

Energy, "dark", p. 25

Enlightenment, p. 79

Entropy, p. 25, 27, 101, 108

Ephrem, St., p. 120

Essenes, p. 46, 68

Eternal: life, p. 39; alternative to, p. 68; concept of, see Eternity; as gift, p. 94; nothingness, p. 68; punishment, p. 67, 90; recurrence, p. 57; and transcendence, p.121-122

Eternity: defined, 26, 113

Ethics, p. 93

Evolution: and change, p. 61 ; and consciousness, p. 52, 57, 102; creative, p.14, 39, 136; culmination of, p. 102; direction of, p. 91-92, 98, 100; defined, p. 18; as designed, p.91; end of, p. 28, 124; evolutionary drive, p. 13-15, 38, 60-62, 63; as "infallible", p. 98; as "irreversible", p. 18-19, 43, 101; potential, p. 73-74, 90-91; and suffering, p. 123

Exoplanets, p. 23-24

Faith: and belief, p. 64, 71-72, 140; and doubt, p.115; as faithfulness, p. 38-39; gospel sense of, p. 71-72, 103; and hope, p. 31-32; leap of, p. 103, 111, 118; risk of, p. 87-96, 111, 122, 138; scientific "faith", see Belief (s), scientific; stages of, p. 64, 136; as trust, p. 36, 39, 64, 71-72, 82, 95, 110

Fowler, James W, p. 64, 139

Frankl, Viktor, p. 64, 82-83, 106, 140

Freud, Sigmund, p. 6, 40, 42, 140; on afterlife, p. 15; on death, p. 38, 66-67; on illusion p. 15, 33; on mysticism, p. 80; and pleasure principle, p. 82-83; on religion, narcissism, and western civilization, p.36; on sexuality, p. 73

Friedmann, Alexander, p. 40

Fromm, Eric, p. 16, 113, 140

Fundamentalism, p. 34, 49, 68

Gautama, Siddhartha (the Buddha), p.58, 121 ; deification p.63

Gehenna, p. 67

Genesis, book of, p. 113-114

God: as "being in itself", p. 66; as creator, p.28; as "Father", p.120, 123; as good, p. 65, 117; as ground of being, p. 14, 62, 66; as "higher power", p. 62-63; patience of, p. 76; as person or personal, p. 63, 71, 89; proof of, p. 79

Goudge, T. A., p.18, 140

Greece, p. 35

Grace: concept of, p. 60, 71, 93-94, 109; vs. works, p. 63

Hamlet, p. 90

Hammarskjöld, Dag, p. 121

Happiness, p. 35; pursuit of, p.82-83, 85

Hawking, Stephen, p. 26, 140

Heaven, ideas of, p. 34, 44, 47-48, 55, 69-70, 113, 116, 121

Hell, p. 37, 65-67, 71, 77, 88-90, 94; St. Augustine on, p. 90

Hinduism, beliefs concerning afterlife, p. 50, 59

Hope, p. 6, 15, 18, 31-33, 36-38, 43-45, 60, 95-96, 101-103, 109-110, 118, 122-123, 125-126

Huxley, Julian, p. 18, 52

Hubble: Edwin, p. 39-40; space telescope, p.23-24

Human nature: Christian views of, p. 47-48; contemporary views, p.49-50; Greek views of, p. 45,-46; Hebrew & Jewish views, p. 45-46; Pauline view, p.60

Humanity, future of, p. 24, 106

Hume, David, p.58

Icarus, myth of, p. 62

Idealism, p.78

Illumination, p.78

Illusion, p.15, 33, 37, 51, 57, 60, 80, 90

Immortality, p.16, 43, 49-50, 57, 61, 80, 92, 100-102, 114, 118, 135

Intuition of being, p.67

Irenaeus, St., p.114

Irreversibility (of evolution), p. 18-19, 43, 101

Isaiah, book of, p. 67

Islam, p. 34, 47, 59

Index

Jansenism, p. 92, 94, 99

Jeans, James, p., 7, 21-22

Jesus: death and resurrection of, p.47, 95, 111; historical, 97; imitation of, p.121; as "Son of God", p.120; teachings of, p. 31, 37, 46, 55, 67, 69-70, 106, 122

Jews: beliefs, 46-47, 59, 69; salvation of, p.70

John the Baptist, p.46, 68-69

John of the Cross, St. (maxims of) , p.83-84, 137

John, gospel of, p. 68-69, 114

Johnson, Mark, p. 9, 42, 138

Jung, Carl Gustav, p. 61, 73, 82, 117, 138

Justice, p. 22-23

Kant, Immanuel, p. 15, 17-18, 39, 138

Karma, p. 75, 89

Kaufmann, Walter, p. 9, 33, 138

Kingdom of God (or of heaven), p. 55, 68-70

Kitigawa, Joseph M., p. 75, 138

Koran, *Qur'an,* p. 47-48

Krauss, Lawrence W., p. 28

Küng, Hans, p. 95-97, 112, 138; re. Teilhard, 96-97

Lakoff. George, p. 9, 42, 138

Lemaître, Georges, p. 40

Le Roy, Edouard, p.102-103

Life span, human, p. 36

Logotherapy, p.82, 137

Love, p.31, 37-39, 93

Maimonides, Moses, p. 47

Mahayana (Buddhism), p.58-59, 63

Maritain, Jacques, p. 67

Martyrdom, p. 34, 37

Maslow, Abraham, p. 79-80, 138

Matter: "dark", p. 25; and energy, p. 49-51, 53; and spirit, p.51-52, 54, 100

Maturity: psychological, p. 73-74; spiritual, p. 74-79

Maya, p. 51

Metanoia, p. 78

Moody, Raymond, p.79, 139

Muslims, and salvation, p. 70-71

Mysticism, p. 81-82; false, p.121

Narcissism, p.36

Near-death experiences, p.80-81

Negentropy, p. 27

Nephesh/Nefesh, p. 45, 60

Nicene Creed, p. 120

Nietzsche, Friedrich, p. 16, 57

Nirvana, p. 58-59, 121

Non-attachment, p. 59

Origen of Alexandria, p.65

Omega-point, p.92, 107

Paradoxical intent, p. 82-83

Pascal, Blaise, p. 5, 39, 87-97, 139; "second conversion" of, 117; Pascal's "wager", 87-97; Küng's acceptance of, 95-96; Teilhard's recalculation of, p. 99-103

Paul, St.: on eternal loss, p. 34, 67; on faith, p.71-72;view of human nature, p.60; on resurrection, p. 32

Peak-experiences, p. 79, 115, 138

Person, personhood, p.35-36, 48-52,; immortality of, p. 102, 107; and reincarnation, p. 50-51; and spirit p. 98

Peter, St., second epistle of, p.114

Pharisees, p. 46

Physics: 24-25; Einstein's, p.52; Pascal's, p.90; quantum, p. 28

Piltdown Man, p. 99

Plato, p. 26, 36, 139; on good, p. 117; on soul, p. 45, 47,

Puligandla, R., p. 50, 89, 139

Punishment, p. 35: eternal, p. 65-66, 88

Purgatory and purification, p. 74, 76

Rahner, Karl, p. 5, 94, 137-34, 139

Randall, Lisa, p. 25, 140

Rees, Martin, p. 14, 22, 140

Reincarnation, p. 8, 50-51, 65, 75

Religion: origin of, p. 44; and Darwin, p. 11; and death, p. 119-119; dogmas, p.72; Frankl on., p. 82; Freud on, p 33-35;

Index

Jung on, 73 : and love, p. 38; and morality, p. 93; and spirituality, p. 76, 85; "New Age"-, p. 76

Resurrection: of Christ and the faithful, p. 32; concept of 46-48; spiritual interpretations of, 52, 93, 111

Revelation: Christian, p.108, 117; Book of, p.113, 115

Reward(s), p. 22, 33-35, 37, 82, 88, 122

Risk: of faith, 5, 88-92, 96, 111, 122, 138; scientific, p.30

Rome, p. 35

Ruach/Ruah, p. 42, 60

Sadducees, p. 46

Sagan, Carl, p. 28, 140

Satan, salvation of, p. 65

Schweitzer, Albert, p. 121

Sheol, p. 67

Second Vatican Council, p. 5, 70-71, 94, 128, 140

Self: -awareness, p. 53; -centeredness, p. 35, 85 ; consciousness, p. 35, 52-53, 57, 60, 66 ; -deception, p. 77; -destructiveness, p. 35 ; -doubt, p.111; -forgetfulness, p. 33, 59; -identity, p. 45, 50, 52, 56; illusion of, p.60-61, 64; -improvement, p. 78;-knowledge, p.77; -transcendence, p. 83, 122

Sinanthropus, p.43

Skepticism, p.56

Smith, Wilfred Cantwell, p. 64-57, 140

Socrates, p. 36

Soul, p.5, 12 33-38; contemporary concepts, p. 49-52; existence questioned, p. 57-58; natural immortality questioned, p.8; Teilhard's views, p. 93, 102; traditional ideas, 18, 44-47; world-soul, p. 92

Spinoza, Baruch, p. 26

Spirit: Holy-, p. 60, 68, 70; human, p.5, 43-45 and matter, p.48-52, 54, 100, 102

Spirituality, p. 53, 59; and religion, p. 76, 85; and security needs, 64, 136; stages in, p. 64, 75, 77-81, 85

Stars, p. 24-25

Stenger, Victor J., p. 28

Sufism, p.59

Sun, age and stages, p. 22

Survival: chances of, 109; of fittest, p. 14-15, 19, 61, 101; of life, p. 23, 95; of soul or spirit, p. 7, 18, 43, 92

Suzuki, D.T., p. 84-85

Taylor, Charles, p. 6-7, 140

Teilhard de Chardin, Pierre, p. 5, 14, 43, 99-104; on "death barrier", p.107-109; views on evolution, p.15, 43, 52-53; on hell, p. 68; on matter and spirit, p. 52-53 ; on Pascal's wager, p. 90-92; 1934 "profession of faith" p. 97-98; published works cited, p.140-135; on the nature of soul, p. 49, 93; on survival of spirit 43, 49, 97-98; on suffering and death, p. 107-109, 122-123; influence on Vatican II, p. 94

Teleology, p. 14

Telos, meanings of, p. 32

Testaments: comparison of, p. 35; Old (*Tanach*) p. 38-39, 70, 137; New, p. 60, 69, 95

Theopoesis or *theosis,* p.115-116

Theravada (Buddhism), p. 58-59, 63

Thomas, Gospel of, p. 55

Thoreau, Henry David, p.123

Tillich, Paul, p. 66

Time and eternity, p. 26, 75, 110, 113

Tipler, Frank, p. 57-58, 135, 135, 141

Transcendence of self, p. 83, 122

Trust (see Faith)

Unitarian-Universalism, p. 65

Universalism, p. 125-30.

Union, unitive stage (with God), p.77-78

Universe: age of, p. 24; defined, p. 28; future destiny of, p. 6-7, 19; other universes or "multiverse", p. 26, 29, 41; shape of ("flat", open vs. closed, oscillating, etc.), p. 25-28; survival of, p.30; understanding of, p. 39-40

Vairayana (Buddhism), p.59

Vitalism, p. 14

Wild, Robert, 9, 144

Index

Wisdom (of Solomon), book of, p. 46
Wolpe, David, p. 47

About the Author

Richard William Kropf, born in Milwaukee, Wisconsin, in 1932, was ordained a priest in 1958 for the Diocese of Lansing, Michigan. He served as parish priest for a number of years, then specialized in philosophical and systematic theology, earning doctorates in philosophy and theology at the University of Ottawa and the Université St-Paul in Canada. He also has engaged in research both in France and Israel. After a number of years of teaching philosophy, religious studies, theology, and psychology in various Michigan colleges and seminaries, he retired to live a life of prayer and writing in northern Michigan. In addition to maintaining a website at www.stellamar.net, his published works include the following books:

Teilhard, Scripture and Revelation: A Study of Teilhard de Chardin's Reinterpretation of Pauline Themes. (Cranbury, NJ: Associated University Presses, 1980)

Evil & Evolution: A Theodicy. (Associated University Presses: Cranbury, NJ, 1984: Second edition, Eugene, OR, Wipf & Stock Publishers, 2004)

Faith: Security & Risk: The Dynamics of Spiritual Growth. (Mahwah, NJ, Pauist Press, 1990: Eugene OR, Wipf & Stock Publishers, 2003)

The Faith of Jesus: The Jesus of History and the Stages of Faith. (Eugene, OR, Wipf & Stock Publishers, 2006)

(with Joseph P. Provenzano) *Logical Faith: Introducing a Scientific View of Spirituality and Religion.* (Huntington IN, I-universe. 2007, 2009).

Views from a Hermitage: Reflections on Religion in Today's World. (Latham MD, Rowman & Littlefield, 2008. Second edition, Johannesburg, MI, Stellamar Publications; 2016)

Breaking Open the Creeds: What Can They Mean for Christians Today? (Mahwah NJ, Paulist Press, 2010).

Forever: Evolution and the Quest for Life beyond life (Johannesburg, MI, Stellamar Publications, 2012, 2014)

Einstein and the Image of God: A Response to Contemporary Atheism (Johannesburg, MI, Stellamar Publications, 2015)

A Journey into Solitude: From Priest-Professor to Hermit-Heretic (Johannesburg MI, Stellamar Publications, 2016)